MW01251525

ACHIEVE WITH GRACE

A guide to elegance and effectiveness in intense
workplaces

THERESA LAMBERT

Fallon Publishing

Contents

Definition of Graceful High Achiever

Graceful High Achiever (n.) a poised and successful person who radiates a balanced and captivating energy; a person who seeks to achieve greatness yet does not measure themselves by external factors and validation; displaying "pretty agility" while savoring each moment on this incredible journey we call life.

Praise for Achieve with Grace

"Achieve With Grace resonates with truth, vulnerability and inspiration. Yes, it is about your career and leadership, but what it is really about is finding the truest meaning in your life, the one that may be hidden behind the expectations of others. Theresa's voice rings clearly and authentically throughout, and it is easy to see how she helps so many people to achieve a state of balanced energy and elegant results. It is so rare to find a book that inspires, motivates, and is also so incredibly doable. Achieve With Grace is not just for the stressed out over-achieving leader.....it is for all of us!"

- Fiona Douglas-Crampton President & CEO of The Dalai Lama Center for Peace & Education www.dalailamacenter.org

"Theresa's focus on Self, Intention, and Energy is spot on. The success you want on your own terms is achievable with Theresa as your guide. Her experiences, achievements, and personal learning create compelling reasons to reflect and take action."

- Jennifer Campbell, Coach, Facilitator, and ImpleMentor creating change in people and organizations www.actionimpactmovement.com

"Highly actionable and accessible guide for self-management results. Theresa provides an insightful and easy to implement approach to achieving your Life's Vision."

- Wendy Leggett, Sales Manager and Business Coach

"This is a book about action with intention. We all seek more balance - Theresa flips the concept of balance on its side and shows us that we are the architects of our life. There are practical tips and thought-provoking questions for those of us who want live with more grace, less hustle and still be impactful in their career and life!"

- Julie Pecarski, BA, RHN

"Making the hardest jobs look easy is reserved for distinct personalities and top performers. Theresa's principles, teach driven people, who are outliers or rebels like her, to achieve success in the toughest situations where grace and poise are necessities."

- Mike Skrypnek, six time author, international speaker and business coach, CEO and Founder of Grow Get Give Coaching www.GrowGetGive.com

"Theresa Lambert's "Achieve With Grace" takes us through a powerful, relatable and immediately actionable coaching model. Leaders committed to effectiveness and balance must read this insightful book."

- Caroline Bagnall - Profitable Hospitality Strategist, Adult Educator www.connecthospitalitystrategies.ca

"While the quest to create work-life balance may be impossible, Theresa illustrates through her own story that work-life integration is achievable. We can be more fulfilled and productive in all areas of our life, when we prioritize self-care, which Theresa defines as self respect. When we take care of our body, mind and spirit first, we are able to show up in our

careers and relationships with a sense of vitality and grace, and with an energy that inspires others. The great John Maxwell says "A coach is someone who goes before and shows the way"; thank you Theresa for sharing wisdom from your own journey and guiding us along ours. Keep shining your light!"

- Megan Dell, Certified Health Coach, dōTERRA Wellness Advocate, Former Hospitality Colleague of Theresa, Mother and Wife www.megandellhealthcoach.com

"Theresa's experience and passion make her the right person to educate you on taking charge of how you spend your time. Her method will teach you how to slow down to get ahead and the world is lucky to have her knowledge captured in a book."

- Blair Kaplan Venables, Best Selling Author of Pulsing Through My Veins: Raw And Real Stories From An Entrepreneur, Founder of the I Am Resilient Project and President of Blair Kaplan Communication www.blairkaplan.ca

"Theresa's motivational guide will serve as a wake-up call to leaders living with constant burnout. These pages serve as a mirror, allowing the opportunity for powerful self-reflection and accountability. Her transformative tools will help shift your mindset and actions to make room for the best version of yourself."

- Joanna Jagger, MA, CPHR, President & Founder of WORTH Association, Capilano University School of Tourism Convenor & Instructor www.worthassociation.com

"Genuine, Candid, Relatable. Theresa understands the challenges of being a professional leader and the expectations that not only our work environment, employees, guests & customers demand but the expectations we also place upon ourselves. Through her three step process, Theresa

shares how professional leaders are able to show up for themselves first, while still achieving their best results on a daily basis."

- Paige Green, Quality Assurance Manager, Diamond Resorts International

"This book dispels the myth that success can only be attained through self-sacrifice, long hours and an uncompromising focus on results. Instead, Theresa Lambert provides proof that self-care and values play a pivotal role in building a life that highlights thriving versus striving. She mixes inspirational storytelling with practical advice on how to change your trajectory from burnout to achieving with grace."

- Cathy Goddard, Business Coach and Mentor Program Facilitator, Founder of Lighthouse Visionary Strategies www.lighthousevisionary.com

"Theresa leverages her own hard-won insights as a highly successful yet burnt out general manager of a top boutique hotel to lay out a practical recipe for thriving as a high achiever. An excellent guide to creating a professional life filled with success, contribution and fulfillment."

- Donna Horn, Leadership Coach and Consultant, Inspiricity Consulting and Roy Group Leadership Inc.

"Having had the pleasure of working with Theresa, I'm excited that she is sharing her incredible leadership with the world. This book is a poignant read at any stage of your career and will most definitely leave readers with things to think about and key takeaways to alter thought patterns right away for positive change."

- Lindsey Turner, Brand and Business Strategist, Bold Ink Strategy www.boldinkstrategy.com

Hire Theresa

"You have to become obsessed with caring for yourself in order to generate the energy to show up fully and take responsibility for your life's direction; this starts by investing in your growth both personally and professionally. If you have productive energy you will have incredible clarity. If you manage your stress, you will be able to make decisions from a position of strength and positivity not fear."

~ Theresa Lambert

∼

Theresa Lambert is an author, transformational coach, mindset strategist, motivational speaker, facilitator and practical intuitive guide. If you are ready to accelerate growth both personally and professionally for yourself, your team or your organization, look no further. Theresa is the ideal person to deliver a keynote at your next event to inspire positive change.

To book Theresa to speak or as a Coach or Consultant, contact:

Theresa Lambert
Theresa Lambert Coaching & Consulting Inc. Whistler, BC
theresa@theresalambertcoaching.com
www.theresalambertcoaching.com

Change Your Story, Change Your Life

"Change your Story, Change your life."

~ Deepak Chopra

As Deepak Chopra said, the formula is simple: when you change your story, you change your experience of life. And at the heart of this transformation is where you'll find "you".

It may sound simple but it took me a while to crack the code and shift from "always *on* and always achieving at all cost" to achieving with grace, balance, and ease.

If implemented correctly, these steps will help you follow your unique path and forge ahead, regardless of uncertainty and without the stress and overwhelm that once ruled your life.

This 3-step process works together in synergy and by the end you will understand that you *are* the person who creates your experience — you are in the driver's seat.

You don't need to be rescued, you don't need to be right, you don't have to do anything you do not want to.

What follows is a process of both self-exploration *and* self-expression. The more masterful you become in each area, the more your life will shift. This is "Self-Management" Mastery at its most distilled.

World renowned leadership coach Brian Tracy said, "Everything you ever are or ever will be is entirely up to you". This is my method to help you become the version of "you" that you want to be!

Step # 1 Story

Self-Management Mastery starts by creating awareness around who you are at your core. This is not about what you do, where you work, or what you own. You are NOT your results. You are the only person who can do what you do, the way you do it.

In order to change your story, you have to first understand *what your story is,* what parts you want to change, and where you want to go.

This step is about gaining clarity and defining *how* to use your inner drive to achieve as a catalyst for positive change and growth.

Step # 2 Intention

Once you have clarity and awareness around your story, thoughts, feelings, and behaviors, it's time to become intentional around how you will put the new vision into motion.

You do this by becoming intentional around how you spend your time, who you spend your time with, how you show up for yourself and others, and ultimately, how you make conscious decisions to move towards the direction of your choosing.

Bringing intention to every moment of your day is like having an invisible compass; your decisions are driven by intrinsic motivation.

Step #3 Energy

This is the step that weaves it all together. *You* are your number one asset, if you take care of yourself, you can take care of others, your business, and be the brilliant leader you were destined to be.

You have to become obsessed with caring for yourself in order to generate the energy to show up fully and take responsibility for your life's direction. If you have productive energy you will have incredible clarity. If you manage your stress, you will be able to make decisions from a position of strength and positivity — not fear.

When we focus on doing things that energize us and let go of the stuff that doesn't, it's the most incredible needle mover we will ever experience.

The SIE Coaching Model

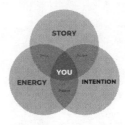

The SIE Coaching Model in Bullet Points

Story:

1. You are NOT your results.

2. Create powerful self-awareness around how your thoughts, words, actions, and behaviors shape the outcomes you create.

3. Be curious about who you are and get crystal clear around what outcomes you want. The relationship you have with yourself is the most important relationship you'll ever have.

Intention:

1. You are in charge of how you spend your time —choose wisely.

2. Break your Big Vision into tiny, tangible goals so small until the impossible feels possible. Don't forget to celebrate them daily.

3. Self-Care is Self-Respect — how you treat yourself teaches others how to treat you, so pay attention!

Energy:

1. The world belongs to the *Energetic* — so focus on doing things that bring you *energy* and let go of everything else.

2. Slow down to get ahead.

3. Surround yourself with people that matter to you and lift you up.

Ready to get stared?

Graceful High Achiever

"I didn't really know what I wanted to do, but I knew the woman I wanted to become."

~ Diane Von Furstenberg,
The Woman I Wanted To Be

The greatest compliments I have ever received were the ones that spoke to my captivating energy, not the ones that praised my achievements. On this journey we call life, even in the short time I've had, I have learned that the only thing in life we can control is how we show up and respond to what life offers up to us. Becoming a Graceful High Achiever is about your ability to adapt and step into the beautiful and powerful woman you desire to become.

It's about channeling your inner strength, your values, your uniqueness and turning it into a catalyst for living your best life on your terms. If you implement the steps I share in this book correctly, you can reach the 7 traits of highly effective Graceful High Achievers:

1. Action: Graceful High Achievers are ready to go at any point in time. They pick a goal and then they take *Action*.

2. Vision: Graceful High Achievers are incredible at setting a clear vision for themselves and others. There is nothing more important than the path to achievement — and it is clear for them.

3. Focus: Graceful High Achievers know how to stay focused. They understand that they can't successfully chase and catch two rabbits at the same time; especially not in an elegant way!

4. Discipline: Graceful High Achievers are incredibly disciplined. They implement habits they know will help them excel and feel amazing.

5. Faith: Graceful High Achievers have a faith that they will succeed. They keep a positive attitude and they're determined to achieve success on their own terms. They believe they will come out on top of whatever they put their mind to, and they have the patience to let the pieces come together naturally to get to the finish line and come out on top.

6. Mindset: Graceful High Achievers love learning how to develop and improve their skills. They know that to be their best, they must look for ways to improve their performance or implement new habits to help them succeed. Having a growth mindset is part of who they are.

7. Value: Graceful High Achievers love to give more of themselves than expected. They will create things that make the world a better place. This innate drive for adding value leads them to serve others. They will move mountains to make this happen.

The barrier to achieving these traits only exist within your mind. You are a powerful creator. One of the things I have heard many times after working with my clients is that I helped them give themselves permission to be who they are and take courageous action based on their desires.

I'd like to invite you to give yourself permission to see new possibilities and to use this book as an inspiration to become your version of a *Graceful High Achiever*.

Introduction

My Story

"The whole point of being alive is to evolve into the complete person you were intended to be."

~ Oprah Winfrey

As a woman in business I always felt incredible pressure to be "successful". The drive to achieve came from the need to feel worthy, to show the world that *I could do it*. That I was *capable* of creating amazing results. That's how it all began.

I totally believed that hard work, long hours, chronic stress, and exhaustion were the price I had to pay for the success I craved. I had bought into the myth that somehow, to succeed in life, we needed to make sacrifices in other areas of our lives. That having a fancy title and earning a really good salary would actually make me happy.

My high achieving inner self was chasing results and recognition. It was chasing this idea of finally being *enough* and deserving of success. So I set out on a path to achieve greatness in my career, I wanted to get there fast… and, I did!

By the time I was only twenty-nine, I was offered a General Manger position at a luxury boutique Hotel in Whistler, British Columbia: a 77-room boutique lodge located in the stunning village of Creekside along the shores of a beautiful glacier-fed lake.

It was incredibly serene and luxurious with oversized suites, grand fireplaces and architecture that hit the balance between rustic lodge and contemporary lines perfectly.

The second I saw it, I wanted to spend as much time in this beautiful space as I could. It actually reminded me more of a stately home than a hotel, which made it even *more* special. It reflected my personal style to a tee, natural but elegant. I felt right at home.

However... from a business perspective, the place was a bit of a mess! Throughout my tenure as the General Manager, I had the honor of building up the business and turning it into one of the top properties in North America, winning accolades and awards. I am a big believer that your people are at the heart of any successful business in hospitality. By putting together a strong team and implementing the right tools, we created an effective workplace culture. This ultimately enabled us to establish a world class hotel.

I poured my heart and soul into this business and it became my greatest obsession. People still ask me to this day how I did it. It felt *amazing* to be able to make it to that level at such a young age *and* to be celebrated for it. But this high intensity environment combined with the pressure to perform that I had placed on myself was enough to drive me to exhaustion. Hitting burnout only 3 years into this role, I knew I needed to find a way to achieve greatness in a way that felt more graceful. I call it graceful because nothing elegant was ever accomplished in a rush.

Here was my predicament...

Keeping it all together to continue looking like a poster child of success while feeling like a hot mess on the inside. My days were a constant fight. Chased by emails, hotel guests, employees, and that endless to-do list... I was *always* on the go, *always* doing something. And, I was terrified that if I stopped I would lose everything I had worked so hard for. I kept telling myself that this is the *only* way. But when I hit the last stage of burnout and let stress rule my day, it became too much to handle.

Being a true service industry professional, however, I had long ago learned that even when there is a fire in the kitchen, the guests can't know about it. So I continued to keep up appearances, putting on a brave face while struggling through my day.

I would go to sleep exhausted and wake up exhausted. I would work weekends to catch up on anything I couldn't get done during the week — yet it seemed like it was never enough.

As a high-achiever I loved to be busy. In fact, if you are a high achiever, then busy is likely your status quo, too.

But, what I've learned over the past decade of transforming the way I work, manage teams, and coach my high-achiever clients, is that if the ability to produce results is your most prized possession than this becomes your greatest gift *and* your greatest pitfall.

Apart from the incredible ability to produce results, the inner drive to achieve can push you to your max until you reach burnout or loose motivation, whichever comes first.

It's the reason you miss family dinners, that yoga class you promised yourself, or back out of a trip with the girls (or boys) again! It's the reason you are a badass and the reason you have no balance. It's awesome and it sucks at the same time.

You love it and some days you hate it because you wish you could just stop and be okay with what you've built thus far (remember weekends?… just saying).

~

Without a doubt, my life experiences made me strong and prepared me to be steady as a rock in the most intense situations, but for too long my "ying and yang" were not balanced.

As the ancient Chinese philosophy suggests, I did not have "qi" (balance). "Yang" is the active aspect of this duo while "Yin" is the receptive part. They are seemingly contrary forces that are actually complementary to one and other.

I have often heard them expressed as the male and female forces. What I recognized is that the achiever part of me is a very dominating "yang" force, more masculine than feminine and as a woman, if not balanced right, it will drain my energy. (And by the way, this applies to the gentlemen of the world too).

This is the exact problem us achievers have. The "Yang" has strength and power to push through almost anything, it can manage chaos, challenges and high-pressure situations, it works brilliantly well to get you ahead, achieve results, lead teams in intense workplaces *and* gets you to just keep pushing.

But when things do not go right, fast enough, or when people and external circumstances beyond our control get in the way of progress, even the most motivated high achiever can get triggered.

It's the trap of getting stuck in reactive mode, a brilliant breeding ground for frustration, burnout, and overwhelm. In this state, if not managed and balanced correctly, it causes you to temporarily lose control, it blurs your vision of the future, it effects the ability to think and act rationally and impedes the ability to create the desired results (or see the results you have created).

This state of being stuck in reactive mode opens your mind to negative thoughts — it blocks the ability to focus on positive results.

It causes all the positive traits of high achievers to be masked by the overpowering emotion of overwhelm, anxiety, anger, doubt, or sadness. As a result, it triggers achievers on a level that effects their personal identity. It triggers questions around self-worth.

As high achievers we are natural "doers", we are energetic, strategic and inherently curious. We love interesting challenges that let us work hard while trying to find ways to express ourselves. We are natural leaders, entrepreneurs, innovators, and developers.

These traits can cause us to have more ideas than we can handle at once which moves us into an "always on" or the constant "what's next?" mode in which we will not stop our pursuit of something until it is done.

Heading for burnout may as well be the title of this chapter of your life (as it was mine) because that's precisely the reason burnout is also known as "overachiever syndrome".

But what drives us to want to "overachieve"? Good question.

Everybody is afraid of something and while it may appear that achievers just go for it and get the job done, they have an underlying fear that drives them to push beyond their max capacity. For some, it is the fear of rejection, for others it's the fear to lose their sense of safety, and for others it's the fear of not being enough, to not be loved and heard or seen in a way that they desire.

It's the dragon you need to learn to slay, it's the reason you keep pushing even though *you know* you need a break, it's the reason you won't ask for help when you know you need it the most, it's the reason you won't let others see your vulnerability. This is the secret shame of high achievers like you and me; we have an invisible armor so thick that most people will never get to see who we *truly* are.

How do I know? Because I am an expert in procrastinating life through busywork and I know what it's like to be a poster child of success on the outside while feeling like a hot mess on the inside. To always wear a mask, to look like you have your shit together when you don't. And, I can tell you… it's exhausting!

What's more, it is stopping you from reaching your full potential and achieving a higher level of performance. When I finally let go of the "active" doer side and embraced silence and calm I found my feminine power, the grace and elegance of moving more gently, more intentionally, more at peace.

It was the "Yin" inside of me that was ready to shine and be embraced. And, when you do things that are aligned with who you are innately, embracing all the parts, both the active and the passive, the yin and the yang, the male and the female, and combine them with your vision, purpose, and passion, you become unstoppable. But it's a journey to get there.

As Oprah put it, the whole point of living is to evolve into the person you were intended to become. It starts by facing our ghosts, gaining clarity on our present moments and creating a vision of our future so big it feels impossible to get there until we finally grow into the person we are meant to be.

I invite you to join me on a journey of self-discovery. Having spent the past three years studying human behavior and whole health, I found a way to embrace who I am and what I need while still going after those big goals of mine. I found a way to celebrate the results without measuring my self-worth against them, and you can do the same.

There are 3 key areas we will take a deep dive in:

1. Your Story: you will gain clarity on what triggers you to push too hard, who you truly are behind your results, and your vision for your future.

2. Your Intention: you will learn my methodology for how to manage three critical resources: time, relationships, and yourself.

3. Your Energy: you will get tools to help you bring energy into five critical areas of your life so you can show up in the way your life deserves (no excuses).

∿

The key to everything you will learn is taking action (this should come easily to you!) and committing to showing up consistently. Nothing in life lasts if we do not make it a habit and we can only become masterful in the art of self-management if we practice it.

Whether your achiever self is pushing you to your max some of time, most of the time, or all the time, if you implement the tools I share with you correctly, you will be able to transform your experience and lead from a place of purpose, strength and positivity. Friendly reminder: YOU ARE NOT YOUR RESULTS, so let's get started!

Part One

ONE

What's Your Story?

"I am who I am. Not who you think I am. Not who you want me to be. I am me."

~ Brigitte Nicole

When you ask most people who they are, they will tell you what they do. There are few people in the world who are brave enough to ask themselves this freaky yet deeply philosophical question, "Who am I?".

Using myself as my own test subject, I began by asking myself this question: *how can I live the life I want while doing the work I love?*

What I learned along the way is that it starts by gaining clarity on who we are and what drives us. Not what we do or how many things we have — surprise! This, in turn, requires us to become hyper-aware of the story we tell ourselves as well as the triggers that push us beyond our max capacity. If we want to create long lasting change, reduce stress and anxiety, and finally smash that vicious cycle of pushing past our limits (or stop feeling unsatisfied with what we've built) we need to *fully* understand *how* we operate in our daily lives. We need full disclosure, transparency and powerful self-awareness of everything that goes on in our mind and body.

The Brain: we are who we believe we are

Did you know that your brain cannot differentiate between your imagination and what actually happened? This means that essentially, if you have a vivid imagination and the capability to create a vision, your brain will consider whatever you dream up as something that in fact… happened!

Coming back to the question of who we are, it's easy to see now that the answer is *really* that we are who we believe we are. When I work with my clients, I like to explore things such as personal strengths and values, but in the spirit of keeping this book focused on the juiciest parts, let's talk about something that you won't hear very often:

 You are in essence a combination of all the stories you tell yourself about what you can or can't do, how you feel, how you react to anything that happens, and the consequent meaning you make of it, also known as your beliefs about yourself, the world, and others.

For example, if you tell yourself that you are not a good leader because your team doesn't follow your direction, then this will be the reality you live out. If you tell yourself that you are always busy, your calendar will be jam packed, you will say yes to everything (even things you don't want to do) because that is the only way you are able to be who you say you are. In this case, you said you are a "busy person", so you made yourself into one.

Lastly, if you tell yourself that you *are* your results, then your sense of self-worth and self-esteem is directly linked to your results. Consequently, you *must* deliver results or you are at risk of a very turbulent dark patch in which you beat yourself up heavily because, without results, you do not add any value.

Turning this into a positive, if you tell yourself that you *can* accomplish anything you want, you actually *will* be able to do it. You will become a person who can do anything. If you believe that you are kind and caring, you *will* be kind and caring. If you believe you can stay calm in intense situations, you guessed it, you *will* be a calm and kind person in any situation.

Turns out in my case, my misconception of myself was causing *all* sorts of trouble for me, including freaking out over stuff that really did not matter. I'm not proud to share this, but honesty will set you free. And by the way, it's an energy drainer not to, so you might as well do it.

WHENEVER I WAS NOT able to keep up with my own unreasonable expectations, I made an assumption about what a colleague was thinking about me or my decisions, I believed that I *must* not be good enough. This belief that I was not good enough, in turn, caused me to self-sabotage my progress, to not take action where I needed to, or to drown myself in busywork because working more equals more success — or at least that's what I believed.

No surprise then, that this pattern caused anxiety and stress to take over and lead me down a rabbit hole of working myself to exhaustion over and over again. I was worried about *all the stuff* that had not yet happened while questioning every conversation and decision I made. I was wrestling with both the past *and* the future while being completely disconnected from the present.

Meet the "Master of Catastrophe"

Also known as the Vortex, the Rabbit Hole, or Last Place On Earth you should spend time dwelling in. Who is this Master of Catastrophe? Well, it's that Inner Critic that blows small meaningless situations completely out of proportion.

Here's a great example of this: in my early years, when we hit work milestones, I would get *super* excited. I would often share key wins with the owner of the company — and I all I wanted was recognition for a job well done.

Often I got back a response that had nothing to do with my original message such as: "I'll be up Friday, let's talk".

But didn't you see how amazing this win was?

Where is the recognition for all the hard work?

Complete devastation on my end — of course! Here are just a few sneak peeks into my dysfunctional Master of Catastrophe thinking of the time:

Email: Trigger

Reaction: "I must have done something wrong" (breathing increases)

Misguided Thought: "I've missed the mark *clearly*. This will be the week I'll get fired." (elephant sitting on my chest)

Misguided Belief: "*This* is the proof, okay now I am freaking out. I must be in trouble! I'm going to loose everything! I *knew* I wasn't good enough for this!" (feeling upset, angry, frustrated, guilty)

Misguided Action: Work harder. (saying yes to more = I'm contributing, I'll be good again, I'll be better!)

Consequence: Long day, bottle of wine, shitty night of sleep, dwelling in despair…

Reality: It's Friday and the owner arrives. Everything is great. He just had a new business idea! Oh? So I'm not fired? (shoulders relax slightly, I must have gotten away with it!)

Takeaway Thought: "Why did I do that?" (there must be something wrong with me, the cycle begins again…)

Mmmmh…. *Really?* Is this all necessary? Well, the answer is of course, no!

WHAT I LEARNED over the past three years of research and experience about our human nature and physiology is that the stories we tell ourselves — especially the ones we self-identify with — shape our thoughts, our actions, and our behaviors.

There is an incredible function within our brain called the RAS (Reticular Activating System). It's like the most amazing coffee filter in the world. It is responsible for filtering all the information that comes in — but it only shows you the most important pieces of information according to your bias. That means you only interpret information based on your pre-existing beliefs which come from past experiences.

What *this* means is that if we tell ourselves we are busy, overwhelmed, exhausted, in trouble, or that our efforts are no longer enough, our RAS will go ahead and make decisions to _support_ this idea and furthermore to find _proof_ that what we believe is actually the truth. This is obviously detrimental to our happiness and mental health!

Having this knowledge is *powerful*. But it's not all bad news. The exciting part is that our RAS is actually within our control. And *because* we control it, we can make choices that support us in changing how we view what's happening in our lives and who we are. What's more, we can create an experience that is *more* supportive of what we want. This means finding a way to have something called *sustainable success*. Moreover, it allows us to create the results we want while understanding that we are not our results.

THE EASIEST WAY TO rewire your brain for success is to focus on the *feeling* you are seeking. Visualize for about 30 seconds how having this feeling would change how you handle certain situations and notice the shift that takes place within you. Go on, try it!

I can tell you that when I started to visualize feeling steady and calm, after just a few weeks, I stopped reacting to emails and was able to simply look at them for what they are without feeling the need to *catastrophize* everything. (Bye bye Rabbit Hole. Hello awareness.)

Our journey begins when we understand and build awareness around the stories we are telling ourselves and shift into what we truly want instead.

TWO

Start Before You Are Ready

"If we wait until we are ready, we'll be waiting for the rest of our lives."

~ Lemony Snicket

By late 2013, I had been with the hotel for just about three years. In this time I had seen three male middle-aged General Managers come and the final one was about to go. Add to that, The Lodge had been through years of turbulence with both ownership *and* management companies changing regularly.

Throughout those years, I had worked my way up to become the Operations & Revenue Manager, overseeing the Rooms Division. The constant changes, different expectations, and perpetual drama that was floating around the place had taken its toll on me. To make it worse, the reputation of The Lodge within the Whistler Community had made staff retention a challenge.

I dealt with a lot of problems on an ongoing basis. It was frustrating because I craved direction and stability. Don't we all? I had been looking for a new role within the resort, but didn't get any of the jobs I applied for. I guess the universe had bigger plans for me...

After the third General Manager left, I was hoping desperately that we as a team would get a new leader who would *finally* work on the culture and bring this gorgeous property to the level of service it deserved.

In the interim, as the most Senior Manager on site, I was asked to step in temporarily. I said yes but was convinced that within a few months a new GM would be found and life would go on. But, just a short time later, the owner of the hotel offered me the position full-time. To be blunt, I thought he had lost his mind.

I mean, I *know* I had accomplished a lot with the company and I had made *huge* improvements where I could. But... me... running a hotel? With no degree or experience? And after I'd seen three people fail before me? That seemed completely insane. So of course I said *YES!*

The way I figured it, there were three options I had in front of me. Go all in and a) actually make it work by building up the culture and business, b) mess it up terribly and get fired (but gain the experience regardless), or c) the golden mean, keep it the same and likely get still fired (but still gain the experience).

So I started before I felt ready — despite the chaos that ruled the building — and I forged ahead courageously. Little did I know, I was about to create a huge success story, both for the hotel *and* for myself.

Let's face it. None of what I share with you and nothing in life can become a reality if we do not take action!

Having dwelled in perfectionism for too long, it's easy to not start doing something because you are afraid you might fail, get judged, or be rejected. Too many of us have attached our self-worth to external factors and outcomes to the extent that we have become terrified to do, say, or risk anything that may shatter our sense of place in the world (More on this soon, I promise).

The idea of starting before you are ready has become a huge part of how I live and I truly hope you can adopt it as well. It can be a bit of a leap because we all have three basic needs that must be fulfilled: to belong, to be safe, and to be loved. So starting before you are entirely ready can throw up some red flags of resistance in your mind — that's *okay*.

What I learned during my time studying at the Health Coach Institute is that the reason for this resistance is because of the way our brains are wired. Information comes in through the senses and gets placed into three 'buckets' ("Three Brains" according to the Health Coach Institute) which all are responsible for different functions of the body. Each of these "brains" has a different set of instructions all geared towards keeping us safe. Let's look at them:

The Cortex or "Human Brain"

The Cortex deals with the logical, human, conscious mind. This is the part of our mind that justifies our choices and behaviors and makes meaning out of our feelings and experiences.

The Limbic System

The Limbic System is in charge of generating emotions. It uses these emotions to promote a sense of safety and wellbeing. These emotions drive us toward (or away) from experiences that establish or threaten love, safety, and belonging.

Brain Stem or "Critter Brain"

The Critter brain is in charge of physical functions: your heart rate, breathing, blood sugar – anything to do with keeping you alive. It's constantly taking a recording of your entire neural system and categorizing it in terms of risk vs. safety. The Critter Brain does not like change. It gets pretty set with what it knows and likes to have those same experiences over and over again. Anything new gets coded as unfamiliar. Unfamiliar = risky = unsafe.

Source: Health Fit Coach, "The Three Brains"

YOU MAY HAVE GUESSED this already, but when we are deciding to start something new, our Critter Brain sends signals that tell us to stop because… it is not safe!

This is where you have to learn to *build* the muscle of "being comfortable with the uncomfortable". I love this because it is *such* a challenge — but at the same time, nothing truly worth pursuing feels comfortable when you do it for the first time!

So, every time you take action, you are leaning into being comfortable with being uncomfortable. And that takes practice! But it's worth it. It will help you break through bad habits, start that project you've been meaning to do for years, launch a business, apply for a promotion, ask someone on a date, or have a tough conversation.

It's a life changer really. I never would have said yes to the GM role if I had waited to truly feel ready. I never would have started my business if I would have waited to be ready to go out on my own. And, I am *sure* you would not be reading this book if I had waited until I was ready to write it.

If you go with the motto, "progress trumps perfection" you can actually start to take action towards the things you really want to do *and* you will satisfy that need to achieve because you are "doing" it!

THREE

Digging Out The Roots

"Real joy comes not from ease or riches or from the praise of men but from doing something worthwhile."

~ *Willfred Grenfell*

I n order to move forward and go from purely achieving to creating balance and achieving with grace, we need to dig a little deeper. As I mentioned earlier, what I realized over ten years of managing teams and coaching ambitious people is that most achievers seek self-worth and meaning from external sources.

I would dare to say that this is actually true for the majority of people. If you grew up with the traditional "punishment and reward" system, I would guess that you will self-identify here. This is a serious problem and if you can't let go of it (or at least loosen your grip of it) then a transformation will only be partially possible. The choice is entirely yours.

MAKING a living is very much focused on creating external success. It's about constantly asking *"what's next?"* and the idea that once we achieve that goal, we move up a level. (This is another story we tell ourselves.)

> The formula of how we live our lives goes something like this: once I have (X), I get to do (X) and then I will be happy, satisfied, and fulfilled!

It is a *nonsense* idea that in order to feel happy and satisfied with life, we need to *have* something first. The truth is, if we are only chasing making a living, we are not creating a meaningful life.

Think about your life for a moment. Look back at everything you have done and just scan the choices and sacrifices you have made. No doubt there are many. But in general, were those choices based on wanting to make a living, or were those choices based on creating a meaningful life?

I RECENTLY READ an article in Forbes Inc. that introduced me to the concept of "praise addiction". The article summarized the main points of a book by Alfie Kohn, Punished By Rewards, which explores the long-term effects that being "over-rewarded" can have on a person's ability to be happy. Here are journalist J. T. O'Donnell's key takeaways:

- Incentives (like praise) are external motivators. They are bribes designed to get us to behave a certain way.
- As a culture, we've been conditioning ourselves over the past 50+ years to seek these bribes in the form of

grades, stickers, trophies, and, yes, praise. It's called "extrinsic motivation".

- Over time, a person can become obsessed with seeking extrinsic motivation. In the extreme, he won't want to do anything until he knows the reward for doing it.
- Being extrinsically motivated can create a barrier to success. Those affected are held hostage by the need for bribes.
- Eventually, a person can lose his ability to be intrinsically motivated to do things simply for the satisfaction of accomplishment.

What I recognized is that because our inner achiever loves accomplishing things, it's easy to get addicted to the bribes available from our world today. They are brilliant motivators because we've been conditioned to believe that "the more we have, the happier we are".

Once I started to pay attention to this, I could see it within me and all around me. People were unhappy but they would choose not to do anything about it. People were exhausted, stressed, and stretched thin, yet they kept sacrificing personal time, energy, and happiness in the name of success.

A study released by The Telegraph found that 69% of people feel trapped in their routine and 40% of people reportedly are unhappy with their life in general.

Being busy has become a badge of honor, and it shouldn't be. Take a moment and reflect on your week. How often have you shared with somebody that you are stressed or super busy when asked simply, *"How are you"*?

. . .

DROWNING in mindless busywork and feeling as though we can't ever get ahead inevitably triggers us to feel uncertain about the future.

There are millions of people in this world who believe that chronic stress and exhaustion are business as usual. And many of them feel trapped in a vicious cycle. So, what does it take to turn this ship around? What would it take to help us understand this is NOT normal? How could we change our ways while remaining highly productive and wildly successful?

Yes, I like to be successful and if you're reading this, I think you do too. But in order to break free from what I call "recognition addiction" and the need to chase external results, we need to start looking at the lies we tell ourselves. We need to pull out this deep root that somehow our worth is measured by our results and by external things we possess. It's simply not the case.

FOUR

You Are The Creator Of Your World

"Nothing exists in our world that does not first exist in our mind."

~ Marie Forleo

When I was sixteen years old, I told my mother I wanted to move to Canada. That same year, I decided I wanted to become the General Manager of a hotel. The magic of the *perfect hotel stay* had always mesmerized and intrigued me. I didn't have *the how* exactly, but I had the end goal. And as you know by now, both actually happened about a decade later.

Back then I saw myself as the GM of a Four Seasons Hotel — little did I realize that I fit much better into a more entrepreneurial environment, but hey, we live and learn!

 When you are connected to a bigger vision, when you lean into your dreams and desires and take *action* despite risk, you generate an incredible amount of energy and the people around you can feel it.

While I am not a person of particular religious affiliation, I *do* believe that greater forces surround and support us constantly. Combine this with the way our amazing brains function, and we have a true match made in heaven designed to get us anything we truly desire — *if* we use it properly. (By the way, if the concept of desire intrigues you, I'd highly recommend reading Think and Grow Rich by Napoleon Hill).

OUR MIND IS the most powerful tool we possess. When we use it to our advantage, it can lift us up, create wild success, and it can instill an inner drive that is otherwise impossible to replicate.

I didn't always believe in myself and in fact at times I have been my own worst critic. But I always had an ability to imagine what else might be possible for me.

Over time, I learned I could visualize things working out for me, especially when I really desired something. My inner critic became more quiet and my goals became more attainable.

Believing you can do something starts with a clear vision in your mind. The more you practice this, the more you'll start to believe in yourself. Knowing what you want and committing to it is a powerful practice. It doesn't often feel comfortable but it is what we must do.

We *all* have something special inside of us. We *all* know what it is, but only a few of us dare to act upon it. A brilliant example of this is Roger Bannister. On May 6, 1954, Roger was the first person to run a 4-minute mile. Many told him leading up to this day that it was simply not possible and that this was an unbreakable barrier. But he believed he could do it! Well on that day, of course the man did it! Within only a few months of his success, many other people followed. Roger had opened the floodgates to break this barrier, he had become a leader in his field, and you can too.

SO START to create awareness around the meaning you make of external success, how you react to other people, and anything else that goes or doesn't go your way. Then, journal! Write that stuff down somewhere and write it down often.

Awareness of what's happening in your world, how you react, and knowing what you want is the first step on this journey, without it, you will not be able to create a calm approach to leading yourself or a team through intense situations. It's as simple as that! Final thought: if you are not your results, then who are you?

FIVE

Fight, Flight Or Freeze - Meet The "Stress Response"

"You have power over your mind - not outside events. Realize this, and
you will find strength."

~ _Marcus Aurelius_

Over the past few years I have become increasingly interested in the effects of stress on our bodies and what we can do about it. Having worked in the hospitality industry pretty much my entire adult life, stress was something that became a part of my and other people's lives. It is talked about daily in this field, as it is in many others I am sure.

It's no surprise really, in hospitality, that workers are under constant surveillance. If you lead teams, you are being judged by your boss, co-workers, and your subordinates, too. And, of course, it's all about "the experience" you create for your valued guests.

There are few jobs in the world in which almost every client (aka the guest) is willing to share their opinion on how you should do your job. There are also few professions in which customers expect you to be fully available 24/7. Why is that? Well, we all travel, we all eat in restaurants or visit a lounge, so consequently most of us believe we have the knowledge on how to run hospitality establishments.

As a former hotelier I'd say that this isn't the full truth, but then again, constructive feedback is critical, so I understand that it is needed. I do believe it's valuable to help improve services and experiences, I just wished people would know the difference between feedback and criticism.

I RECALL an incident in my early hotel years that happened to a colleague of mine. A guest had returned from an evening out and attempted to get into his room (or so he thought). He kept coming back to the front desk and demanding a new key. Each time he returned, he became increasingly aggravated. With his last attempt, he stormed towards the desk and started to scream at the front desk attendant that this was the worst hotel he had ever stayed in and that clearly nobody knew how to run an establishment.

He then threw the key card in my colleague's face and screamed at the top of his lungs. There were other guests nearby who watched in shock. A third key was made and it was decided that a Bell Attendant would accompany the angry guest back to his room.

The key worked of course and the guest seemed very confused. Turns out, he had tried to access his room… from the wrong door.

When I arrived for my shift the next day, I found a message from my colleague who shared that she was shaken and wanted to chat about this incident. There were also two voice-mails. One was from the guest who had caused the incident — he apologized for his behavior. The other was from a guest who had witnessed the incident and was offering to act as a witness should we choose to report this incident to the police.

The moral of this story is that not everything is always as it seems. While I have heard the words "the guest is always right" a million times, sometimes a guest is simply wrong. There are lines one shouldn't cross, and on this note, kindness will never go out of style.

The good news is that we learned a lot from this incident. We added protocol that if a guest returns or contacts us a second time about a key issue, we'd send somebody along with them.

All good things. But the stress and anxiety that this incident caused was long lasting. So next time you want to scream your head off at a front desk agent, think again. Your feedback is valued, if it is given with the right attitude, but please refrain from causing employees unnecessary stress and anxiety, they are only human after all!

~

THE DICTIONARY DEFINES stress as "a state of mental or emotional strain or tension resulting from adverse or very demanding circumstances". The moment stress is activated our heart rate speeds up, blood pressure increases, respiration quickens, adrenaline flows, non-adrenaline and cortisol are released, our digestive system shuts down and blood flow is re-routed to the arms and legs!

Why does this happen? The combination of reactions to stress in our body evolved as a survival mechanism, enabling our ancestors and other mammals to react quickly to life-threatening situations and perceived danger. Thanks to the perfectly orchestrated sequence of events within our body, sending blood to our limbs (and with the bonus of the release of adrenaline) this allows us to temporarily use our limbs to their full capacity and *literally* run or move faster than we could otherwise! This in turn allows someone to fight the threat off or flee to safety. Pretty awesome I would say.

So in a time before any of us were born, the ability of our body to detect danger and turn on the stress response was literally a life saver! When our ancestors found themselves being chased by a lion, they had a better chance of survival due to this response. You may wonder at this point why the hell I am bringing this up... truth be told while our brain is an incredible operating system, it cannot differentiate between REAL and IMAGINED stress! The stress we experience today equals the stress our ancestors experienced. Our body changes its focus from thriving to surviving mode.

Ok, I am going to say this again because this is critical: our brain cannot differentiate REAL and IMAGINED stress.

Let's dive a little deeper. This means that every time you are feeling stressed by tight deadlines, expectations of others, expectations of yourself, maybe after making a mistake, getting yourself "in trouble" or feeling like you are not showing up enough (or perhaps you are not even sure anymore *why* you are feeling stressed) your body has turned on the stress response and put you into "fight or flight" mode.

Your Sympathetic Nervous System is on high alert and firing on all cylinders — you may notice shortness of breath, tight chest, racing heart beat, restless legs, foggy brain, as well as heightened emotions.

And when this becomes chronic, you are in trouble and you will no longer be able to respond in a graceful and effective manner. This is the reason so many people snap, react, make poor business decisions, and generally end up feeling miserable. And remember, the point of this book is to help you navigate that, so let's not lose focus.

≈

FOR ALMOST EIGHT YEARS, up until January of 2018, I was in a high stress, high intensity, high pressure environment, most of which I put on myself willingly. And, I could feel the effects on my body as I tumbled towards complete burnout.

(By the way if you're interested in knowing more about the effects of stress on your body, head to my website at Theresa Lambert Coaching and sign-up for my newsletter — you'll get access to my ebook on managing stress — and some other goodies!)

WHAT I HEAVE LEARNED over the years is that most stress we experience is really just us trying to control other people's actions or external circumstances — all things that are far beyond our control.

A key part to understand here, is that most stress we experience today is caused by our mind. The great Stoic Marcus Aurelius knew this a long time ago. When we start to recognize that we have power over our mind and that we can control how we react to things and how we feel about external circumstances, we will find great strength. The sooner you realize that *you* are in charge of your experience, the sooner you will feel more calm and collected.

This in turn will allow you to achieve all you want with grace and ease! Bringing this back to the story I shared about my colleague, she had a choice to make: should she hang on to that intense situation, continue feeling anxious (or even worse, feeling responsible for that guest's anger) or should she let it go and choose to learn, take some deep breaths, move on?

∾

BREATHING IS one of the best and most underrated stress management tools we have! Two minutes of deep breathing is proven to calm your nervous system. Next time you feel stressed, put a timer on for two minutes and take some deep breaths. Focus on your breathing, notice the inhale and the exhale. Take note of how you feel.

Our goal here is to achieve with grace, to be effective, and to react thoughtfully to intense situations. To do this we must understand what causes the stress, gain awareness of what or who we are trying to control, and accept that the only thing in life we *can* control is how we respond. When nothing is certain, everything is possible. You are the master of your mind, use it to your advantage.

SIX

The Golden Mean Philosophy aka.
Defining Balance

"Virtue is the golden mean between two vices, the one of excess and the other of deficiency."

~ Aristotle

W hen it comes to balance, it's not about finding it, it's about creating it. You've just learned about the brain and the body's function to deal with your vivid imagination of what's happening in your life. Now let me give you a tool that can help you on your path to creating the kind of balance that can *finally* move you forward.

When we learn from our problems, they become the gift to help us solve our biggest challenges. They teach us to temper that part of ourselves that tirelessly pursues goals and to do it in a way that is sustainable and empowering. It's about living a life on your *own terms*. It's about managing your "achiever self" in a way that helps you crush your most important goals — while taking charge of your time — and slowing down enough to care for your overall wellbeing. It's about embracing the yin and the yang to find a golden balance point. And when you do, you move into your optimal achiever zone. This optimal achiever zone is what I call "self-management mastery".

∽

WHAT I LOVE about hotel life is that no day is ever the same — it's the perfect playground for a type A personality. In any hotel, each day is like a surprise party — some parties are delightful, and some are an absolute disaster. What follows is not one of those delightful stories...

During one of my first years as the GM, I remember we had all eagerly prepared the hotel for the upcoming winter season. In Whistler, B.C. this means high rates and high occupancy mixed in with high expectations from guests. Due to the seasonal nature of Whistler, it *also* generally means that half of the work force is new to their roles — most of the employees have never even experienced what "busy season" actually looks like.

So here we were in one particular year, thinking we are ready to go when all of a sudden, about ten days before Christmas, the parking lot floods due to high amounts of rain. This causes the water to make its way into our main guest elevators... causing them to malfunction and forcing them to be completely shut down!

Umm... what the hell?

How are we going to deal with this? Why now? How do we tell the guests that they have to haul their luggage up massive flights of stairs? Now, you might think everyone would understand and be kind and patient, but you would be wrong...

I learned that in these situations, it's best to apply The Golden Mean Philosophy: find a way to solve the problem as soon as humanly possible *and* manage expectations along the way. In this particular case that meant go for full disclosure sweetened with a small offer to soften the blow: breakfast for everyone until the elevator is fixed! (Costly but who doesn't like a lovely meal, right?).

Was this the perfect solution? Nope. The perfect solution would have been to get the elevators fixed in one minute without even one guest finding out. Even *more* perfect would have been if none of the staff had to know about it either, quite frankly. That would have been magical! What I found instead was the middle ground: the *perfect-not-so-perfect-plan* to deal with uncertainty and mitigate disaster.

Staying calm and patient while experiencing stress is a moving target, but a worthy one. And it takes practice to nail it.

While some guests were quite understanding and thrilled about breakfast, others were upset and vocal about "this being unacceptable". I totally agree, it wasn't great, but understanding that this was beyond my control helped me keep my calm. This was the best solution that I could come up with. It wasn't perfect but we got the elevators fixed just before Christmas and life went on. That's the thing, life *always* goes on.

∽

ARISTOTLE, a great philosopher and hero of mine, believed that virtue is moral excellence. A virtue, according to him, is valued as the foundation of principle and good moral being. He believed that personal virtues are characteristics valued as promoting collective and individual greatness. Pretty deep stuff! (But highly applicable in today's world).

I was introduced to his "Golden Mean Philosophy" during my time studying Philosophy at the University of Stuttgart.

Aristotle defined twelve virtues that marked the centre of a sliding scale. He believed that we either have a *deficiency* or an *excess* of each particular "virtue". Therefore, living in a way where you are centered would enable you to live a "good life".

One of the twelve virtues I consistently see in High Achievers is courage. According to Aristotle's scale, an excess of courage makes us *reckless* while the absence of courage renders us a *coward*. Therefore, true courage is the balance point between recklessness and cowardice. Our goal then is to practice this virtue at the balance point between the two.

My experience with Aristotle's work became a way for me to view the world and determine the value of my actions and behaviors based on this sliding scale. I encourage you to read up on him and other great minds throughout history. You might find something that resonates with you and guides your approach to modern life.

As a driven and ambitious person, creating success and accomplishing things on a day-to-day basis is critical to feeling whole and satisfied. When we achieve the right amount each day, we feel happy and fulfilled, but if there is a deficiency, we fall into despair mode.

On the opposite side of the spectrum, when we obsess over achievement, we have the tendency to burn ourselves out because the mission to achieve becomes bigger than anything else. This causes us to let other areas fall to the wayside and, over time, it can be destructive to our health and our relationships. So we need to aim for *just the right* amount of achievement each day to be centered in this golden middle.

We are all unique and so with this said, take some time to apply this philosophy to daily decision making — start with something simple such as compromising with co-workers.

Next, you'll learn how to supercharge your momentum by gaining clarity on the meaning and beliefs that drive your behavior. And when you can do that, my friend, you are ready for the next step: let's get *intentional*!

Reflection to Action Challenge Part I

To help you take action on your journey to Achieve With Grace, let's recall the first step in the SIE Coaching Model: Story. This is a critical first step to self-management mastery and it starts by creating awareness around who you are at your core.

Focus: this is not about what you do, where you work, or what you own. You are NOT your results. You are the only person who can do what you do the way you do it.

In order to change your story, you have to first understand *what your story is*, what parts you want to change, and *where* you want to go. This step is about gaining clarity and defining how to use your inner drive to achieve positive change and growth.

Start by thinking about your life for a moment and answer the following questions:

1. What assumptions am I making that cause me to feel stressed or anxious?

2. What do I think supports this experience?

3. How does doing these things make me feel?

4. How would I like to feel instead?

5. Visualize: if I could feel the way I want, how would it change my situation? (Hint: write it down, write it down, write it down.)

Let's dig a bit deeper. Now that you have clarity around your assumptions and how they cause you to feel out of alignment, let's challenge your thoughts and beliefs.

1. What lies am I telling myself about my life or myself?

These are your beliefs. Think of your inner voice — what are you telling yourself about your life, your choices, your responsibilities etc.

For example, "If I say 'no' then I am a bad person" or "I have to work harder than everyone to prove my worth" or "I am always busy!"

Be honest! If you have trouble with this exercise, simply spend the next seven days and just notice thoughts that come up…

2. What do I believe external validation and praise will do for me?

3. When I feel as though I am *truly* contributing, what is it that I am doing?

4. How do I feel when I am contributing and doing things that I want to do, compared to when I feel I *have* to do something?

Let's bring it together to give you focus.

1. Which beliefs or assumptions cause me the *most* stress right now?

Try to pick only one and remember that a Graceful High Achiever knows that she can't chase two rabbits at once.

2. Close your eyes and sit with this thought or assumption for a moment. What do I see myself doing or not doing? How does it make me feel?

3. What would be possible if I could let go of this belief or assumption?

4. Look at the possibilities that you just wrote down. What is a short term goal that you could set today to help you move towards this?

5. Think of what you are good at — things that come naturally and easily to you, your personal strengths — What strength could you use to help you achieve this goal?

6. Having this knowledge now, what is it that you *truly* want and truly feel 100% committed to moving towards?

What's a golden nugget that you are taking away from Part I? Write it down and I'll see you in Part II!

Part Two

Introduction

"Be the change you wish to see in the world."

~ *Mahatma Ghandi*

If you've worked through the first chapters and have taken the time to self-reflect, you should be starting to understand yourself and your actions a little bit better. The next part of this book will teach you how to break down your big goals into manageable tasks *and* remind you to celebrate them daily.

Remember: you cannot manage your Graceful High Achiever effectively if you do not have *clarity* around what is happening in your life, what causes you to feel overwhelm, and who you are innately. You are in charge of how you spend your time so choose wisely. (A good deal of this time should be dedicated to understanding what makes you tick, by the way.)

∼

The second part of the S.I.E. framework is Intention. There are three precious resources that we need to get *intentional* about as Graceful High Achievers in order to succeed. These resources are:

1. Time

2. Relationships

3. Self

Yes, this next section is all about intention as it relates to you, but you'll *also* learn the truth about self-care, what you're teaching others about how to treat you, and why you need to detox dangerous personalities from your life in order to build your dream team.

SEVEN

Your Time

"Time is the most valuable thing a man can spend."

~ *Theophrastus*

W e all have the same 24 hours in each day, yet *how* we use our time and *what* we do with it is where things differ greatly. When it comes to time, you have to determine how you can use it to achieve maximum results in the most effective way.

One of the greatest insights I was ever given was the 80/20 rule (also known as the Pareto Principle). The belief here is that 20% of what we do yields 80% of the results. So, if we believe this to be true, and personally I do, then we waste 80% of our time doing mindless tasks that pretty much lead nowhere. My Graceful High Achiever self simply can't stand for that!

I'd like to think that if we are more strategic and set the right intention, we can create an experience in which we have "spaciousness" in our lives (time to just be) rather than wasting it doing nothing which of course leads to nowhere.

AFTER I BURNT out three years into what I thought was my dream job, it pushed me to look at how I spend my time. I'm a hands on, learn-by-doing kind of leader. You could always find me in the trenches, helping out wherever I could. I did this because helping others and being of service to someone else gave me a sense of meaning and satisfaction. However it *also* caused me to spend a lot of time doing things that did not yield impactful results.

Gaining clarity on the actions that created results versus the ones that did not allowed me to hand off tasks that really did not have to be done by me. In other words, delegate!

As a *solopreneur*, this same principle also allows me to gain clarity on what I need to focus 80% of my time on as well as the things I should spend only 20% of my time on.

 Whether we spend time doing something or doing nothing, that time is irreversible. It's gone for good.

We can't go back and change time which is why it is so critical that we get intentional about how we want to use our time (stay tuned to learn all about taking "think weeks" later!).

The best way to manage this precious resource is by creating a solid plan around specific goals. If we want to achieve our most important goals, we need to stop wasting time on things that do not matter and instead focus our time and effort on the things that do. Here's how...

Plan Your Work & Work Your Plan!

A goal without a plan is like a sailor without a compass: guaranteed to get lost at sea. Unfortunately, it's not enough to just know generally *where* you want to go. If you don't spend time focusing on creating a roadmap to help you get there, you will spin your wheels. It's mindless action.

Will you get somewhere without a plan? Potentially, yes. But it's guaranteed to take longer and you will experience many detours along the way.

Personally, when I am not strategic or intentional about how I am going to get from A to B, the goal will often fall to the wayside and get lost along the way. I have done this time and time again, especially in regards to my health — and I think we all have. I would commit for a short amount of time to a new routine and then fall straight back into my old habits...

Remember, the Critter Brain does not like change. What is needed is a plan to execute in a way that helps quiet the Critter Brain. We can do this by celebrating our wins and practicing appreciation for our efforts.

PRACTICING appreciation for our efforts is something that has become chronically absent in our world today.

We have been so crammed full of other people's "overnight" success stories and major accomplishments that we have forgotten to appreciate the small things in life. Learning to celebrate little wins in a big way *and* practicing appreciation is vital to creating success. It propels us to keep going because, let's be honest, impact requires momentum. And momentum requires dopamine.

Wait, what?!

Yes. The best way to tap into our inner momentum is to do things that signal our brain to release the hormone "dopamine". Dopamine is a type of neurotransmitter that sends signals between your neurons and your brain. Your body naturally produces it but so do activities that make you feel pleasure. It helps you to strive, focus, and generally find things interesting.

Putting this into practice, for me, meant actually writing down my goals and dedicating time each week to moving towards these goals, no matter how small.

One of my goals was creating more balance and this meant that I had to establish stronger boundaries — it also required me to put every little thing in my calendar such as dinner with friends, gym time, quiet time, and so on.

This might seem like overkill, but for someone who feels more comfortable "doing stuff", this was my way of keeping myself accountable. And I can tell you that it worked every time. All of the sudden, I went from confirming a meeting at the proposed time mindlessly, to checking my priorities *first* and then responding with a time that suited me *better*. And guess what? Not *once* did anyone question why the proposed time didn't work for me! It was a new experience that opened up all sorts of extra time in my day (surprise!) and I would highly recommend you try it. Now let's tie this back to my friend dopamine...

"It's the small wins on the long journey that we need in order to keep our confidence, joy and motivation alive."

~ Brendon Burchard

When we celebrate wins tangibly (like coloring in a box beside each task on a to-do list) we can *physically* see that we have accomplished something. This releases dopamine. When this happens, we feel motivated. When we feel motivated, we are much more likely to keep moving towards a goal because it gives us a deep sense that we are moving in the right direction. In other words, momentum begets momentum. But it is solely contingent upon celebrating those goals. How fun is that! Here are my top three ways to do this:

- At the end of each day, week, and month, review what you have done and ask yourself, "What's been going well for me?"
- Draw a little empty box beside each task on your to-do list. As you complete tasks, color them in and take a moment to thank yourself for completing this task.
- Congratulate yourself for reaching milestones and create a ritual of some sort. This could mean that at the end of each week or month, you do something that you enjoy. This could be as simple as buying yourself some flowers, getting a massage or taking an extra long walk. Whatever floats your boat!

Developing Your Listening Muscle

A huge part of building relationships is developing what I call your *"listening muscle"*. Most of us feel chronically unheard, under appreciated, or misunderstood. If you can learn to truly listen and build rapport with others, you will be so far ahead of your peers (and the general population) you won't even believe it. And what is even better, is that it's simpler than you may think!

Becoming intentional around the concept of fully listening is a real game changer. Can you recall a time when you shared a story with someone and you felt truly heard and understood? If you have ever had a good coach or a good leader, you know what I am talking about. So how can you practice this for yourself?

> When learning to listen, focus on asking questions versus "fixing or teaching" the other person.

When you shift into contributing "less quantity" and "more quality" to the conversation, you're showing others that you honor the knowledge that lives within them. By listening and asking questions, you get to be the mentor, the knowledge-base, the go-to-gal, the person who shows people the power they have. In short, you get to be the natural leader. And you can use this on yourself as well, by the way, simply by listening to what *you* need! I promise you this is a powerful practice so start training this muscle and notice the shift this creates.

Here's all you need to do: talk less and listen more. Start by aiming for a 40/60 and work your way to eventually 20/80. Leaders listen. Simple as that. People love to talk, and they love to share their stories, so when you learn to listen, you won't believe how much gratitude and appreciation will come back. Not to mention insight!

EIGHT

Your Why

"There are only two ways to influence human behavior: you can manipulate it, or you can inspire it."

~ Simon Sinek

A s Simon Sinek so perfectly explains it, there are only two ways human behavior can be influenced. One of these ways — the right way and the good way — is to inspire change. Personally, I absolutely love this. I don't like doing anything that does not have *some* larger purpose attached to it. So when I started to apply a deeper "why" to my personal goals and desires, it became so much simpler.

Have you ever watched Popeye the Sailor Man?

Well if you haven't just Google it…

Connecting to your *why* on a goal is like Popeye eating his spinach. It gives you super strength. It's like the secret sauce that gets you from being a goal setter to goal getter. It's an indescribable motivation that keeps you going.

I was introduced to the power of *why* through my journey of becoming certified as a Health & Transformational Coach. What I learned during this time was completely life changing on so many levels — I finally came to understand how I can apply *who I am* to *what I do* — instead of letting what I do define who I am.

Confused yet? Here is the thing. If your goal is to create more balance while working a job in a field that believes in over-working, you'd have better luck turning a mountain upside down.

If you are in a role where being completely stressed out is the norm, how can you ever pull back and see the forest through the tree? How can you ever make clear decisions about moving forward and up-leveling your career if you fall into bed exhausted every night?

I have made it my life's work to advocate for change because this way of being is just not sustainable. It's no surprise then, that we are seeing oppositional trends appear within the next generation. They have clearly decided that the status quo isn't working for *anyone's* mental health. We're seeing a rise in the gig workforce, freelancers, work from home, changes to the traditional workplace environment… it's truly a wonderful evolution.

But instead of looking at their attitude with a curious perspec-tive, too often they are labelled as lazy! This is unfortunate because it's easier to judge behavior (fixed mindset) rather than asking yourself what you can learn from this (growth mindset).

I can't tell you how many people I have seen working them-selves into the ground, getting sick and unhappy, and then blaming everything else for their own misery while not taking the next scary step to move on. I've been there. It's no fun.

I realized that bouncing back from burnout while still working as a Hotel General Manger wasn't just about getting healthy again. It was about creating a new way of living that could inspire a powerful shift in all those around me. I wasn't just doing it for myself anymore.

The idea that we can be wildly successful while doing less with *more* intention — this is a powerful realization. That we do not have to be superwoman to feel as though we are making an impact and showing up — this is liberating beyond imagination.

But the shift didn't come easy...

Trust me when I say this, there were times that were *tough*. But knowing the importance of becoming a role model and inspiration for how we approach careers was huge to me. Making the last step to choose to pursue my own business full-time was fueled by the same *why*: to impact more people and to do what I love.

Helping other ambitious, driven and smart leaders break that damn cycle of busy and overwhelm and reclaim their time, sanity and energy is my life's focus. To inspire change – to be a true leader in the way that I show up for myself and for others, inspires me to create impact far beyond my own life.

 Strength grows in the moments when you think you can't go on, but you keep going on anyway.

NINE

Breaking Your Big Goals Down Into Manageable Steps

"The secret of getting ahead is getting started. The secret of getting started is breaking your complex, overwhelming tasks into small manageable tasks, and then starting on the first one."

~ *Mark Twain*

S tarting anything new *already* comes with the challenge of getting buy-in from your Critter Brain. Next, you've gotta *lean into* discomfort.

Blegh!

Who wants to be uncomfortable?

I will admit it. The concept of leaning into discomfort took me a while to accept because of my previous mindset. But my previous mindset was destroying my health and sanity, relationships, and overall quality of life. So rather than aiming for quantum leaps, I needed to adjust and break down complex goals into simple steps. Next, I needed to focus on achieving each step, one at a time.

I began by breaking my big goals down into **5 magic moves** or milestones. From there I would focus on gaining clarity on what I needed to do that month, that week, that day. This essentially means that I take a lot of small steps each day that ultimately lead me to my big goal.

By doing this it is much easier to stay focused and motivated while navigating the inner critic. Moving towards your goal every day by accomplishing small tasks makes it both easier *and* exciting to accomplish things. Let me give you a very simple example of this.

Let's say you want to lose weight. You currently weigh 170 lbs. and you want to get down to weigh 150 lbs. If you aim to lose 20 lbs. in 1-2 months it's unlikely, quite frankly, that you will make it. Unless you go on a crash diet (which we all know doesn't work) so either way you're bound to fail.

Instead of crash dieting, let's assume your 20 lbs. is an annual goal. This means you need to lose approximately 1.67 lbs. a month or less than 0.5 lbs. a week! If you think about losing 0.5 lbs. a week, well, how achievable do you feel this goal is now? Quite, I'm sure!

I encourage you to think about your big goals in this way: how much do you need to break it down in order for the steps to feel attainable? What are the different steps you need to take to get there? Write it out. Write it out again. And, you guessed it, one more time. Make each step so small and so achievable that you think, *heck, I can do that easily!*

By doing this you will be able to achieve your goals faster than you could have imagined. Sound simple? Good. It's supposed to be!

Rather than chasing after a huge unattainable dream, you now are *working* towards small realistic goals each day.

Like me… when I wrote this book! Instead of thinking about everything that *needs* to happen, I broke it down into manageable steps. Writing a few words every day versus writing the entire book over a weekend.

The process of breaking down these goals should feel personal. What might be attainable for you may not be realistic on a daily basis for someone else. So work within your timeframe, your expectations, and your schedule. Don't push your schedule on other people as you will surely be disappointed, ask for consideration from others if you feel that you simply can't complete a task in a given timeframe. It's not just the end result that will determine your success, it's about creating a process that is uniquely yours, and that you can enjoy and celebrate as well.

TEN

Your Dream Team

"Find a group of people who challenge and inspire you, spend a lot of time with them, and it will change your life."

~ Amy Poehler

et me start this chapter by telling you a funny story from my time as a General Manager. I have no idea why this is, but the most inconvenient maintenance issues *always* happen when hotels are full. If you have worked in hotels or hospitality, you might know exactly what I am talking about.

On one occasion, we had a leak in one of the rooms and a small (about 3x3 foot) spot was soaking wet. Of course, it was just in front of the closet at the entrance to the bedroom, so chances are, if staying in this room a guest would walk right over it. With only two hours left to the guaranteed check-in time (and after the team had tried to figure it out on their own) I went up to the room to check it out. Wow. It *was* pretty ugly.

So I decided to grab a hair dryer and an iron, and together with another team member, we got to work. Thirty minutes later, the carpet was dry and the mystery spot was gone. The way we show up for others in tricky situations is critical. Sometimes this means getting into the trenches without judgement and just getting the job done.

I like to look at relationships like a really good investment: the more time and attention you give to a relationship (business or personal) the more you will get out of it in return. By showing up intentionally and by being fully present, we can be our best selves as leaders.

Ask yourself how you show up in terms of your current professional relationships with other people, even the tough ones:

1. How do you serve/add value?

2. How do you want to treat others?

3. How will you have built trust?

4. How will you practice appreciation?

5. How will you receive feedback (positive/negative)?

It's important to note that you do not need to lead teams in order to build your dream team. Your team can be comprised of friends, family, mentors, coaches or business partners. It is widely accepted that we are the average of the five people we spend the most time with, so I'd say it is critical that we choose wisely.

This is where intention comes into play...

For a lot of us who work within organizations, we may not always be able to control *who* those five people are. However, who we spend our time with *outside* of work *is* something we can control.

When thinking about who those five people should be, I always choose ones with whom I can be myself. This is probably the most important criteria. Who are the people I can ask for help? Who are the people who won't judge? Who are the people who support me? Ask yourself these questions now and maybe write down the answers, too.

It's important to gain clarity on who you want on your dream team. One or more of them, by the way, may very well be a coach that you pay for and that's okay. I call this having *outside counsel* — someone who will help you see the places you're stuck and give a non-biased perspective of the narratives you are telling yourself.

Close friends and family (or even co-workers) may not be able to see it, or they may not feel comfortable telling us the real deal. It is *so* important to find those five people who will call you out when you need it the most, who will catch you when you fall, and who will pull you back to reality when you are getting lost in your story. It's also okay, for the record, for your dream team to change over time.

REMEMBER that you are not your results, but you will not always see that. Especially as achievers who are driven by the need to feel worthy, we will often get stuck and trapped in our own stories. It is a journey and it takes time to create that change. Heck, I've been working on it for years and still find new triggers to derail me that I haven't yet experienced. When that happens I go straight back to step # 1 – What's my story?

You may have one or two people who are slightly ahead of where you want to be in business — that's good! Observe the way that they care for their body and their mind. Observe their habits and approach to work and to others. Once you've found your dream team and you get intentional about supporting each other and accepting support, incredible things are possible.

ELEVEN

Letting Go of Toxic People

"Your network is your net worth."

~ *Porter Gale*

Something that is critically important but mainly overlooked is cutting cords with toxic people. Sometimes we find ourselves in situations where friendships or relationships with co-workers have turned sour, and even though we know they no longer serve us, we continue to entertain them. Learning to let go or cut people out of our lives is part of the journey to success both professionally and personally.

I LIKE to think about life as a train. During our trip we makes stops, some people get on and some people get off. And then there are those times where we realize that somebody did not pay for their ticket... *this* is when we politely ask them to get off our train.

Some people will stay with us for the entire journey, while others, simply will not. I'd like to believe that they have a better train to catch elsewhere!

By looking at it this way, as much as it may be tough to have a conversation with a friend or person you once loved, it is an act of kindness to set that person free.

You are doing both yourself *and* this person a favor because you will *both* be moving forward productively and healthily. Having tough conversations is important — you'll either resolve what's going on or you will gain the peace of mind that moving on separately is best.

When it comes to managing teams, this is something that as a leader I have learned the hard way. As a compassionate person and someone who recognizes people's contributions, I struggled with this for a long time. I always wanted to believe that people who perform their work at a high level are worth investing in. But the harsh reality is that if you have a high-performing member on your team who is really negative towards others, you need to let go of this individual, and fast.

I have been in situations where I've worked with team members who have caused anxiety, stress, and conflict to others on the team, myself included. When I finally put a stop to it, rather than a collective sigh of relief for me and my team, it actually blew up in my face! Being harshly criticized for not acting sooner, or in some cases, waiting too long to act is never fun, but tough decisions need to be made. But within a short time, your team will recalibrate, everyone will eventually work together again instead of against each other, and life will go on.

 The bottom line is that suffering is optional. Whether in business or in your personal life, you can choose to *not* spend your time and energy on people who are bringing you and your team down. You can choose which relationships you invest in and you can choose whether you want to suffer or not!

We only have so much time in our lives. Be intentional about who you spend that time with and show up fully for the ones you want in your life. Give the relationships that serve you the care and attention they deserve. When you are surrounded by people who lift you up, inspire you, support you (and you do the same for them), you will never feel alone again!

TWELVE

Your Self
_____

"The way you treat yourself sets the standard for others."

~ Sonya Freidman

Becoming intentional about how you show up for yourself, your needs, your desires and your passions is critical. This is where you finally get to build out what success truly means to you.

Remember, you are NOT your results. In the first part of this book, you explored your values and strengths, now you get to create ways to leverage those parts of you that give you your unique superpower.

You might have heard of the saying that you should "treat others the way you'd like to be treated", and I totally agree with this. However, it is a two-way street. What this means is that "you need to treat yourself the way you want others to treat you".

What I have seen over and over again is that high achievers love to jump into action to help out a friend, colleague, or family member because this increases the chances of recognition and praise for them. And, because praise is an addiction, helping and showing up in service to others gives achievers a *genuine* high and a sense of feeling good, feeling worthy, and feeling needed!

All solid reasons for sure, but more often than not it is done with the sacrifice of personal energy and effort. This in turn causes high achievers to become resentful. They start to blame others for taking away "my time" and "my energy" and "my resources". But the truth is, the achievers *ought* to be taking responsibility for making that choice in the first place.

With this being said, the constant "yes" attitude teaches others that we are ready and willing to help at the drop of a hat. So even if people know that we have plans, we've trained others that it is totally acceptable to ask us to change them.

 We often say yes because we are afraid people will not see our value if we say no.

Over my close to twenty years in the service industry I have met many achievers who suffer from the "service sacrifice attitude". This might be so engrained in who you are that changing it feels like you are losing a part of your identity. But you are doing yourself no favors here. There is a reason you are asked to "put your oxygen mask on first" on airplanes!

The truth is that people will actually value you more if you start to set some healthy boundaries for yourself. People will still see your worth and in fact your worth will start to *increase* in the eyes of those around you.

66 This is because you are still able to give superior service and value to others without giving them *all* of you.

What makes this win even sweeter, when you get it, is when you start to show up for yourself in this way you have more to give than you ever had before. This is because you are fresh and inspired, not burnt out and stressed. Showing up powerfully and with intention for yourself is good for everyone.

Your Inner Monologue

It's crucially important to be mindful of the language you are using when you speak to yourself. We are always listening to our own voice, and reflecting negatively on our work and on ourselves has damaging effects. Do any of these statements sound familiar?

"I am so incapable."

"I am such an idiot, *of course* I messed this up again."

"I feel so overwhelmed, I always overload myself, why do I do this? It's so unprofessional!"

"I am so disorganized, no wonder I messed up again."

These are damaging, counter-productive sentiments and the key to being more positive is learning to be *intentionally kind* to ourselves. So, pay attention to how you speak to yourself. It matters!

Let me give you an example that you may be able to relate to. In the first year of my General Manger role, I decided that I must have what I call an open door policy. As such, whenever anyone came into my office looking for assistance, I would make time for them. Even if I had deadlines to meet or an endless to-do list, I would *always* say yes.

While it gave me instant gratification to assist someone in solving their problem, most days I would end up feeling unproductive because I didn't accomplish what I felt I needed to get done. Nobody noticed that I wasn't doing things fast enough or in the timeframe I had set, and yet I was criticizing myself heavily for it.

This negative self-talk was draining my energy and the "yes attitude" was causing me to feel behind. Consequently, I would work late nights and weekends to play catch up. This seemingly small example is loaded full of goodies, and here's why:

First, the story I was telling myself was that in order to be respected and accepted by the team, I always needed to be available. This was exacerbated by my negative self-talk. I was telling myself that I was falling behind and consequently, I created more work for myself all in the name of success. I also taught other people that I was available anytime regardless of how much was on my plate.

To transform this experience, I had to set stricter boundaries. I needed to say no and ask people to come back at a later time — and by the way, I also learned to close my office door.

Key Takeaways

The way you treat yourself is the way others will treat you. If you'd like to have others respect your personal boundaries, you need to respect them yourself. This means you'll have to say no to events, projects, and commitments that you simply do not want to do.

> If you want others to respect you, you need to respect yourself. This will require you to gain clarity around what respect means to you.

In order to do this, you need to be able to express authentically what you need and what you can offer people around you versus focusing on winning their approval. Perhaps that comes in the form of being able to agree to disagree on certain topics while accepting the other person's opinion as valid. Perhaps it comes in the form of you taking ownership of your time, energy, and attitude. Maybe respect comes to you by letting go of toxic people — don't be afraid to kick people off your train!

Ask yourself this:

- What does respect mean to me?
- How do I want to be treated?
- Do I *really* want to help or am I just saying yes to be recognized for my efforts?

At the core of it all is being intentional about what you need. This can be anything from time alone to space to be creative, to have open debates, set clear boundaries, or changing how you talk to yourself and a word I learned to love... self-care!

"Sometimes the hardest part of the journey is believing you're worth the trip."

~ Glenn Beck

I used to throw *such* an eye-roll when some well-meaning friend or family member told me to make more time for "self-care". I don't know about you, but emptying my calendar for *me time* didn't sound like a particularly productive way to get ahead in my career.

I spent years saying that *I didn't have time* to take better care of myself but the truth was that my self-worth was way too wrapped up in my achievements and the validation of others for me to even understand the value of self-care.

Who would I be if I left the office at 5 pm when there was still work to be done? How could I call myself successful if I admitted that I needed extra support on a project? How could I define myself as a leader if I didn't push myself past my limits to reach that big goal?

My obsession with *achieving* was what made me feel worthy. Of acceptance. Of a management title. Of love. Yes, of love. And *that* is the secret shame of achievers like you and me... if we don't pack our calendar with commitments, we feel as though we're being lazy. If we don't check our email before we get out of bed in the morning, we feel like we'll get behind. If we don't say "yes" to everything, we feel like we're missing out on opportunities (or worse — letting others down).

MYTHS. All of them.

There's nothing wrong with being ambitious or driven. In fact, I'll be the first to admit that I still get a ping of pride when someone tells me that I'm working too hard. But the problem is: our productivity is *actually* inextricably linked to self-care.

The more time you devote to your happiness and well-being, the more energy and creativity you'll bring to your work. So making time for self-care isn't just a way to expand your capacity for success without burning out — it's *also* about finding more meaningful ways to cultivate self-worth that aren't measured by external achievements.

Self-care is a practice that looks different for everyone but any way you slice it, it's the highest form of self-respect.

Why do I say that? Good question! Let's look at this from a different perspective for a second. Think of somebody you have a lot of love or respect for. Could be a mentor, family member, friend, idol, anyone. Who is it? (Write it down.)

Once you have the name of the person, contemplate this thought and pretend you are saying this to them: "Because I respect you so much, I will ignore you when you are tired, deny you things you love when you haven't worked hard enough, force you to push harder even if your body is breaking, tell you that you do *not* deserve to take a break. I respect you *so much* that in fact I am going to demand from you that you do everything for everyone else, but you never do anything for you. I respect you *so much* that I want you to drop everything when someone else needs help, because not helping is selfish."

OUCH!

Would you *ever* tell this to *anyone* you love or respect? I sure wouldn't, so why would I restrict *myself* from doing the things I need to do in order to show up as my best self?

Self-worth starts when we respect ourselves and our boundaries.

This is absolutely essential. When we treat ourselves like we are our #1 asset we can start to make powerful shifts that fuel both our physical *and* mental capital. We can make monumental life shifts and show up as our best, most powerful, and most impactful self.

So much of life is simply a matter of perspective and good perspective comes from a positive mindset. In order to have a positive mindset and remain open, we must look after ourselves first.

Reflection to Action Challenge Part II

Let's continue on your journey to becoming a Graceful High Achiever. If you completed the first "Reflection to Action" Challenge you should have more clarity and awareness around your story, thoughts, feelings, and behaviors. Now it's time to become intentional around how you will put this vision into motion.

Bringing intention to every moment of your day is like having an invisible compass: your decisions are driven by intrinsic motivation.

Remember, you do this by becoming hyper-intentional about how you spend your time, who you spend your time with, how you show up for yourself and others, and ultimately, how you make conscious decisions to move towards the direction of your choosing.

To download the accompanying workbook and gain member access to my course "Achieve with Grace 101" head to www.theresalambertcoaching.com/reward.

Enter code: **A3REWARD4YOU**

Now let's build on the work you've done in Part I

1. Think of a goal you truly want to achieve. Write it down.

2. When you imagine achieving this goal, how does it make you feel?

TIME

1. Consider your goal and the feeling that achieving it would give you. How much time would you need to achieve this goal? Does it feel doable in hours, days, weeks, month or perhaps years?

2. If it's years or months, think of breaking the goal down into mini goals. Make them so small that you feel you could achieve them in a week or less. Write this down.

Daily Practice

Commit to completing one step each day to help you achieve the first mini-goal by the end of a week. Ask yourself daily: "what is one step I can take *today* to move me closer to my goal?"

Self

1. What is one thing I can start to do each day that would enhance my own sense of wellbeing and nourish my soul?

2. What do I need to do to make sure I will follow through?

3. Whats one thing that might be challenging but would immediately help me feel as though I have more time and balance?

Daily Practice

Ask yourself, "how do I want to show up for myself today?"

Relationships

This is a Listening Challenge. If you are up for it, spend the next week focusing on listening. Be curious, ask questions. Notice how this changes your interactions. At the end of the week, spend some time and reflect on how it felt different. What did you learn?

Daily Practice

Ask yourself, "how do I want to show up for others today?" (Write it down!)

Toxic People

1. Think of the people who surround you. Is there anyone who is toxic in your life? Write it down.

2. If you have toxic people in your life, how can you let go of them?

3. If you have unavoidable toxic relationships at work, how can you protect your wellbeing?

No toxic people? No problem! Answer these questions instead:

1. Are there any relationships you'd like to improve upon?

2. What could you do to improve these relationships? Tip: listening more might be one of them.

What's a golden nugget you are taking away from Part II?
Write it down!

Part Three

Introduction

"Because everything we say and do is the length and shadow of our own soul, our influence is determined by the quality of our being."

~ Dale Turner

Have you ever entered a room and there was this one person you felt immediately drawn to? They seem to have an incredible aura or energy about them — almost as if they have some sort of magnetic field surrounding them. You can't help but want to know who they are, what they do, what makes them so special. You want to be near them.

To your surprise, when you start talking to them, you recognize you have things in common! But something is still *different* about them. You can't quite work it out, but you wish you could be more like them. To have the same energy and influence. As Ralph Waldo Emmerson said so perfectly, "the world belongs to the energetic" and it's true, captivating people stand out from a crowd.

When I started to realize that my ability to be impactful, influential, and successful was directly linked to my ability to

generate energy — not my ability to create external success —
I *knew* this was the needle mover that would help me create a
major transformation in my life.

I became obsessed with ways to generate energy and it all
began with (scary word alert!) self-care.

I also recognized that I needed to gain clarity around the
things that were *draining* my energy. This included admitting
the biggest lie I had been telling myself for years: that every
minute of every day is about achieving and conquering.
(Wrong!)

Be honest with yourself for a minute. Is this *also* how
you start your day? From a place of anxious energy?

I grew up with the *early bird catches the worm* mentality so step-
ping away from this was not easy for me. But putting everyone
else's needs above my own can only last for so long.

If you're letting others dictate what your priorities will be, how
can you ever start off on the right foot with a productive
intention and an energetic mindset? There is no staying power
to feeling overwhelmed before you've even started your day.

This low energy, high anxious approach turns your mornings
into "rush hour" before your feet have even hit the floor. Not
only is it counter-productive to let others into your mind, it
invariably makes you irritable and impatient towards them.

Create Space

As the boss of Microsoft, Bill Gates took "Think Weeks" a
couple of times a year to create more headspace for big ideas.
He'd escape to a secret cabin, somewhere in a cedar forest in

the Pacific Northwest. Nobody was allowed to visit, this was *his* time and space to be with his thoughts.

He credits a "Think Week" with giving him the space to come up with the idea for launching Internet Explorer in 1995. This is a pretty incredible example of what can be accomplished when we allow our mind the time and space to not just take in information, but to absorb and integrate it into a wider net.

I figure if Bill Gates used a "Think Week" to invent such a vital part of modern life, I needed to give it a shot, too!

When I started to make this small but powerful shift, I realized that some of my best ideas come to me when I'm just sitting, quietly gazing out a window, cuddling my cats and sipping my tea. This practice has improved my creative problem-solving skills as well.

In a world that's hyperconnected by tech, we've forgotten how to connect with ourselves, be alone with our thoughts, and let ideas marinate. We think that we feel energized by doing more instead of slowing down and doing less. And since one of the most powerful skills we can possess as leaders is self-awareness, the practice of being alone is one of the best ways to really flex that inner muscle.

Rather than starting our days feeling under pressure, we need to shift into practices that make us feel a sense of calm and tranquility. We need to do things that make us feel refreshed and productive from the get go. And most importantly, we need to create headspace so that we can see the steps required to show up in our lives. I call these "Silent Minutes" and you'll learn more about this when I dive into faith and flow later in this section.

∼

The quest for *spaciousness* became my word for the year 2019. By focusing on creating the feeling of spaciousness, I managed to have most of the year filled with weekends without obsessing over my phone, a five-week break to get married (all without checking my email even once!) mainly 40-hour work weeks and playing over 60 rounds of golf. I was still the General Manager *and* I was building my coaching practice on the side.

What would have been a big surprise to me years earlier was now nothing but proof that my teachings were working. I did not drop the ball, the building did not catch on fire and ultimately, I finally created enough space to see what was possible for me next. I'd finally take the leap to build my own soulful coaching business. And I dare say it, this is the reason I was finally able to write this book and hopefully like Bill Gate's Internet Explorer, it will open up people's mind to access new opportunities, ideas, and maybe even transform their world.

Even The Energizer Bunny Recharges

Shifting into slowing down, taking breaks and bringing mindfulness to my life was pretty much the opposite of what I had practiced for years.

It wasn't easy. It required becoming hyper-aware of what I was doing, reducing the amount of time I was working, and creating *much* stronger and healthier boundaries for myself in terms of how much I wanted to be connected.

I constantly thought about this one question and used it to guide me: is this giving me energy or taking it away?

THIRTEEN

On Balance

"Balance is the key to everything. What we do, think, say, eat, feel, they all require awareness, and through this awareness, we can grow."

~ Koi Fresco

Creating awareness of our actions, behaviors and thoughts, and how they impact others, is perhaps one of the most powerful tools we have at our disposal. What I love is that this is a tool that *anybody* can learn and that *every* leader should coach their teams on. Heck, every parent should teach this to their kids, too!

Our thoughts, actions, and behaviors are so habitual to us that we often do not even notice when we do or say something biased. But, what is important to know is that our brains and bodies are *"always listening"*. Everything we do, think or say is being absorbed as a cue by our brains and in turn becomes a signal for what our bodies do next.

Our mindset, attitude, and the way we show up for ourselves in our life is tied to the amount of balance we feel we have (or do not have) in our lives.

Ultimately, while we may not consciously know this, we are all in charge of our own experience of life. This means that the stories we tell ourselves about who we are (and who others are) ultimately form the way we experience day-to-day life. To realize that *you* are the creator of your own reality is pretty powerful stuff.

After I learned more about the mind and the power of habit change, I realized very quickly that in order to create more balance, I needed to become hyper-aware of how I was showing up in each key area of my life. The five key areas I looked at were:

- Career
- Finances/Money
- Relationships
- Spirituality
- Health

Specifically, I wanted to explore how I dedicated my time and energy to each of those areas. I wanted to determine if I was showing up in these areas fully, somewhat, or not at all. Once I had gained clarity on which areas I was *not* actually spending much time in, I started to explore which areas I wanted to be more active in.

Breaking it up in this way was powerful. It became very clear to me that there was one area on which I had spent more than 80% of my time, energy and attention: my career. It's not just about where my focus was, it was also about identifying where my focus *was not*.

What does this mean?

It meant that I finally knew exactly *where* I needed to shift my attention. In order for me to create an experience of a balanced and energized life, I needed to put the same amount of work and dedication into other areas such as my health and relationships.

I started to become consciously attentive of how I was spending my time with activities that gave me energy instead of taking it away. Keeping both a mental and physical journal, I started to document experiences that energized me versus experiences that drained me. I also created a catalogue of all the stories that I told myself about my life that stopped me from having more balance. Here are my top three:

- I don't have enough time to do things that I love such as cooking, exercising, meditating, relaxing or hanging out with friends.
- If I don't check my emails first thing in the morning and on weekends and vacations, I will fall behind and something bad is going to happen.
- If I am not the hardest working person in the room, I will get fired.

As I looked at this, I also started to pay attention to what I was doing and who I made time for. This included obsessively checking my emails (every waking hour). Binge watching Netflix or other TV shows for at least 3-4 hours a day on the weekend because I was so exhausted (also called being a couch potato). Let's face it, mindless screen time is a creativity zapper. Especially social media…

I also used work as an excuse to avoid social activities (and then of course I'd berate myself for what a horrible friend I was for never showing up). These are just some of my finest examples, but the list was quite long.

When we start to create awareness of where we use excuses or destructive habits to keep us away from authentic experiences, we have the power to choose a new way!

 Energy flows where the attention goes and the power of choice must be harnessed to create a state of balance.

Life gets simpler when we live in balance. We can start to recognize what causes stress, anxiety, and exhaustion — and we can shift towards what makes us energized, happy and alive!

Once we have this awareness, we can start to implement new habits and behaviors that support the life we want. We can choose to do what *serves* us instead of opting for what holds us back. Growth is rooted in this shift, both professionally and personally. But we can't do it alone…

FOURTEEN

On People

"You're the average of the five people you spend the most time with."

~ Jim Rohn

I ntentional relationships with productive people are the key to elevating your energy. Surrounding yourself with *uplifters* is your best (external) chance for change in the right direction. American Entrepreneur Jim Rohn was the first to articulate the notion that we are the average of the five people we spend most of our time with. Take a moment to think now about the five people *you* spend most of your time with. Is it possible you need a change? Consider the following personality types and how they align with your current crew:

1. The Inspired

2. The Passionate

3. The Motivated

4. The Grateful

5. The Open-Minded

The positive energy generated from inspiration, passion, motivation, gratefulness and being open-mined is infectious! This means that the more time you spend with these five personalities, the more you will feel inspired, motivated, grateful, passionate, and open-minded.

When we spend more time with people who have one or more of these traits, it will start to bring out the same in us. The beautiful thing about this is that, just as when we are triggered by someone's judgment, we can become equally triggered by someone's joy.

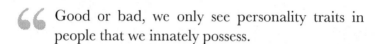 Good or bad, we only see personality traits in people that we innately possess.

So if you detect one of these traits in someone, chances are they exist within you. When you bring positive energy to what you do, you start to become a beacon of light. What's even more exciting is that you pass it on to others. That's the magic sauce, alright!

All the steps I am sharing with you work together. If you lose your way, come back to step number one in the SIE Model. Simply answer these three questions:

1. What's the story I am telling myself?

2. What's the positive intention behind that story? Can I change it? If yes, then how can I make this story work for me? (If the answer is No, it's time to chose to let it go!)

3. What can I do today to help me feel more energized as it relates to my story?

FIFTEEN

On Career

"True leadership stems from individuality that is honestly and sometimes imperfectly expressed... leaders should strive for authenticity over perfection."

~ Sheryl Sandberg

A s high achieving women it appears that so often we are being judged, watched, and measured. This "surveillance pressure" can leave us striving for perfection and setting unreasonably high expectations of ourselves that are impossible to live up to.

The challenge with perfection is that while you may call it "high-standards", it is often the number one reason you drain your energy for your career. This sets you up for the constant chase for more, the never "good enough", the endless journey to achieve perfection. I don't know about you, but just reading this makes me tired.

About three years in to my role as General Manager, my drive for perfection had left me completely zapped. What made it worse was that I had this feeling that nobody ever followed through on their promises and completed tasks to my standards.

I recall one particular moment where one of my leaders passed me in the hallway and said, "You truly are super-woman". She meant it in the most sincere and positive way, but somehow it struck me. For months I had been struggling to keep up with expectations and pressures yet I kept dropping the ball (in my mind) and I felt as though I was looking to everyone else to help me make decisions. The fear of getting it wrong, of not making the perfect judgment call — it was all dragging me down and eating me up from the inside out.

At that moment, I realized that I was role modeling an ideal that truly cannot be achieved. Yes, maybe I was very good at my job, good at creating results, and good at being a leader. But I did it with a veil of "perfection". I was hiding my flaws by showing up powerfully — and it was exhausting.

If I wanted to get my energy back, I needed to let my team members show up in their own way. I needed to show up more authentically as well. To share my struggles and let my team know what was *really* going on so that they could feel empowered to do the same. Because, truthfully, I did not want to be perceived as "superwoman".

While it may have been meant as a compliment, it held a much needed mirror up for me and how I was acting. I needed to let go of the unreasonable expectations that I had set for myself. Maybe I was making it look easy but the truth was that I felt like a hot mess who could not see the success she was creating let alone enjoy it. Things truly needed to change.

~

THIS IS when I adapted the same rules around energy to my career. If it doesn't energize me, I won't do it. Simple as that.

This included saying no more often and challenging the team to bring me answers rather than always offering solutions. I loved coaching them rather than advising them, it energized me so I ran with it. Every time I noticed something gave me energy, I started to do more of it. Conversely, when I noticed things were draining my energy, I stopped or delegated the task to another team member.

The Pareto Principle

As mentioned earlier in the book, this is the idea that 20% of what we do yields 80% of the results. The trick is to flip this equation on its head.

So, if you can work out the part that yields 20% it's no surprise that you'll probably land on the exact same activities that energize you the most. We want to expand that to become 80%.

During my tenure as the GM, I took the property from best kept secret to an award winning, internationally recognized destination. I was also able to build a productive team and increase revenues by over 106%.

Plus, things started to get easier and my last year before taking the leap to self-employment was the smoothest year yet: I had more time, more fun and more trust, all the while doing less and focusing on what energized me *and* driving tangible results.

How is that? Well good question!

Here is the thing: when our goals, values, and behaviors are in alignment, we feel energized by them. A very easy way to gauge if what you are doing is working for you, is to ask yourself: does this energize me? If it is a yes, awesome! You are in alignment. If it causes friction or resistance to your core beliefs, it's time to pivot.

Now, don't get me wrong. In business there will be things that need to get done that you won't enjoy. However, if you can keep those activities to 20% and spend 80% only doing things that energize you, you will ultimately win and feel fantastic in the process.

Plus when you are energized, you can be authentic and have realistic standards, you can be graceful in stressful times and you can create amazing outcomes that move you forward.

SIXTEEN

On Negativity

*"It's not what you say out of your mouth that determines your life, it's
what you whisper to yourself that has the most power"*

~ Robert T. Kiyosaki

T he inner critic that lives between our two ears is the
most powerful energy suck there is. It's the voice that
stops us from taking action, from leaning into our
desires, and from following our heart. It crushes us from the
inside out.

Thanks to the RAS (reticular activating system), confirmation
bias exists which causes us to constantly look for proof that
pre-existing beliefs and values we hold are true.

What does this mean again? Let's recap.

If we believe that we are only worthy if busy, we will fill our
calendars with "stuff". If we believe that carving out time for
ourselves means we are lazy, we will do just about anything to
make sure we never take time off. If we believe that saying no

or rejecting other people's wishes makes us a bad person, we will always say yes to things (even if we really do not want to do them).

These right here are the negative stories that drive our most energetically draining behaviors. Remember, this is what I call the "Story" step in the SIE coaching model. Even though rationally, we *know* that we need to take time out, say no, and stop being "busy", the underlying belief about our own self-worth being tied to this behavior atrophies us.

 But here is the thing, it takes the same amount of effort to fight the old as it does to create the new. The big difference however, is that fighting the old drains our energy, while building the new *gives* us energy.

Remember, our behavior is linked back to actions that make us feel loved, safe, and give us a sense of belonging. Your challenge around self-worth and self-acceptance can be tied to either of these three. At one point or another being busy helped you to accomplish something. It served you. And that's okay. But it doesn't anymore. It's time to move on.

I've been through it, believe me. Accepting that I was innately worthy and that my actions and external validation had nothing to do with my sense of worth was tough.

GROWING up I experienced bullying and rejection — my life felt like a constant battle. Being "busy" kept my mind occupied with other things so I did not ever have to relive the past hurt again.

In 2006 I went on a healing journey backpacking around the world. I had read previously that in order to heal from old trauma, we should consciously replace a past hurt with a new experience. That's exactly what I did and, yes, it *truly* helped. However, my behavior around stuffing my calendar never stopping and the need to always be busy did not stop either. Everything I was doing was *still* linked to this idea that as long as I am busy, I am worthy, significant, and important.

I kept telling myself silently for most of my life that I cannot stop and in doing so, I became a master of *catastrophizing* things.

When managing the demands of my GM role and my personal life became too much, overwhelm sent me into a dark spiral. It tested my relationships, my faith, and my sanity. If I look back, I can see that it was all rooted in negative self-talk. It was time to really look at what was going on. I was fighting with myself and it was exhausting.

Ask yourself... what are the thoughts and beliefs about yourself that are objectively hurtful? When you overload yourself or make a mistake, what's your inner self's reaction to this? Does being overwhelmed make you somehow *worthier* of the career and life you've built? Does this thought make you feel empowered and energized... or exhausted? If it's the latter, it's time to let go.

EARLIER IN THE book I had spoken about checking in on your story and getting clarity around what "lies" you are telling yourself. To help you transition to the next step, I'd like to introduce you to "The Work" of renowned author Byron Katie.

"The Work" is what Byron Katie calls "meeting your internal wisdom" and I absolutely love this. It's a simple and powerful way to tap into our inner wisdom and help "fact check" the assumptions we are making. Often we hear something once (that's all it takes!) and we accept it as a "universal fact" that can easily be used as external blaming.

Using Byron Katie's words to describe this simple yet powerful practice not only helps us remain aware of our stressful thoughts — the ones that cause all the anger, sadness, and frustration in our world — but it helps us to learn to question them. It is through that questioning that the thoughts lose their power over us.

Great spiritual texts describe the what — what it means to be free. "The Work" by Byron Katie describes the how. She shows us exactly how to identify and question any thought that would keep us from freedom. You can find out more about this brilliant human and her life's work here.

And, here are the four powerful questions that will set you on your path to being free:

1. Is it true? (yes/no)

2. Can you absolutely know it is true? (yes/no)

3. How do you react, what happens when you believe that thought?

4. Who would you be without that thought? (or how would you feel if you did not have that thought)?

Sit with these questions, write them down, and revisit them as often as you need to.

SEVENTEEN

On Money

<hr>

"If you're focused on not having enough money, you're going to find ways to not have that money."

~ Theresa Lambert

L et's talk money! If you're uncomfortable, you are not alone! I read an article recently on CNBC that claimed that "Americans would rather talk about anything, *even politics*, over income." It's shocking to me that only about 10% of adults will discuss their income at home.

Millennials are smashing this statistic however with 75% of them discussing money and income at home with their partners at least once a week.

I would dare say that most of us want more money yet we are unable to talk about it. Why is that? I think this is because the majority of people feel as though they do not have enough of it. And this, right here, is the *exact* reason we stay searching when we should be savoring.

Remember, your mind goes where your energy flows, plus your RAS (that killer coffee filter in your mind) will ramp up and amplify your focus. If you are focused on scarcity when it comes to money, if you make it a taboo topic in your home, if you avoid dealing with the relationship you have with money, you will set yourself up to not ever have enough of it.

You will consciously or subconsciously find ways to *not* have enough money, no matter what your circumstance. This could mean you have great wealth in a savings accounts but refuse to go on your dream vacation. Or perhaps you don't have a great income, but you'll spend more than you have in an effort to keep up with The Joneses.

When it comes to money, what is the relationship you *want* to have? Do you want to feel like running when someone brings up the topic of money, or do you want to embrace it?

How you do one thing is how you do everything.

If you have perfectionist tendencies or feel as though nothing is ever enough, this same attitude translates to money.

Energetically you want to start feeling comfortable about money and acknowledge the money you have and will have (and need) in the future. There are endless relationships both personally and in business that are pulled apart by money. This is a choice.

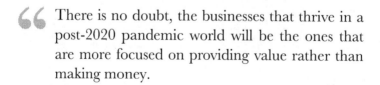 There is no doubt, the businesses that thrive in a post-2020 pandemic world will be the ones that are more focused on providing value rather than making money.

They are aligned with the times and understand that when you offer superior value, when generosity leads, when you are trusting of the process and lean into abundance, people, good fortune, and money will follow.

~

OVER THE YEARS I have started to invest time and money into my personal and professional growth; reaching a point where I spend 5-figures a year (or 10% of my gross annual earnings) on courses, coaching, and other avenues of improvement.

Some people would say this is crazy and not necessary. But here is the thing, every penny I have ever spent in my personal or professional growth has come back to me exponentially. Instead of trying to be an expert at writing a book, coaching, leadership, managing teams or creating epic sales funnels on my own, I decided that I was going to get the help I needed. This way, I could achieve my biggest goals and do it in a way that feels graceful and energetic!

By investing money into my growth, my relationship to money has ameliorated greatly. Money has become a supportive friend rather than an axe hanging over my head. I value the relationship I have with money and in return it values me greatly. The gates are open to both giving and receiving. Instead of sleepless nights and stressing about wanting more, I am grateful for the money I have. In turn, I feel energized and I have enough.

If you want to feel energized by money and be able to give more and receive more, you need to open the floodgates and let money in. This starts by developing a positive relationship to money.

Before we move on let's bust one common myth: "money makes you a bad, greedy and disliked person". Have you heard this one before?

Well I have, and I've heard it from my clients. The ones that have plenty of it, and the ones that would not allow themselves to have it. So let's be very clear here. Money does not change you, it only enhances the qualities that are already within you.

> In fact, nothing in life changes us. Only our reaction to it does.

We *choose* if we want to evolve by learning from the past and focusing on our strengths to move forward, by taking leaps of faith and by leaning into discomfort to break down the invisible walls. But it's important to remember that all that evolving you're doing (all that work on yourself) is not actually changing "you", it's simply enhancing and developing the qualities you innately possess.

If you are a caring, kind, and giving person, money will enable you to express this more through giving. There are many philanthropists who support the arts, innovation, and initiatives that make the world a better place.

On the other hand, if you are an inward looking and greedy person, well, you will just be that and are likely miserable despite your wealth. At the end of the day, ask yourself this: if you could get a cheque for $10 million dollars tomorrow, what would you do with it?

EIGHTEEN

On Faith + Flow

"Faith is an oasis in the heart which will never be reached by the caravan of thinking."

~ Khalil Gibran

There is a warm and loving energy that surrounds us. It guides us, it's the net that catches us if we dare to leap, it's the hand that shows up to help us up after we fall, it's the miracle that happens just when we feel it's impossible to move on. If we have faith, if we are connected, if we are in tune with this energetic life force, we will arrive at the happy and fulfilled life that we've dreamed of.

Some people, sadly, will spend their entire lives draining their energy by worrying about failing. Failing in their relationships, in their careers, as a parent. That worry and fear of failure stops them from ever moving towards what they truly want. It causes them to keep repeating the same patterns over and over again (the definition of crazy). These are the types of people who are not satisfied, who often feel tired and bored with their lives, and are exhausted by the thought of change.

As a natural achiever you have the edge and the opportunity to break this mold, to write your own story and if you believe that it is possible, it *will* provide you with the energy you need to make it through the peaks and valleys to come.

You are not your results.

Embracing and loving the journey while trusting the process is one of the greatest gifts you can give yourself. Your subconscious mind is powerfully connected to the greater forces that surround us. You have everything you could possibly ever need to make your dreams into a reality, but you need to have faith!

Whenever I have let go of my fear or doubt, I am able to do things in a way that feels effortless. From pursuing my dream of traveling around the world (which led me to immigrate to Canada) to becoming a GM at 29, or building a soulful Coaching & Consulting business and now becoming an author. All that hard work would have been useless without the faith to carry me through to the end.

When we lean into faith — both in ourselves and that which is greater than us — the results are incredible. We evolve, we grow, we make our dreams come true. We follow our hearts and achieve success in ways that feel awesome. We are no longer stopped by our fears but instead become driven by our inner guide.

Practicing trust and aligning your faith with the universe requires you to first and foremost practice silence. Why?

Listen to the silence, it speaks.

You need to spend time being with your own energy. Turn inward. You can do this through meditation, writing, or being in nature. But you must do it in solitude and stillness, no tech, no podcasts, no doing, just BE-ing. It's a powerful practice.

I like to practice what I call "Silent Minutes". It's something I use daily and I have taught it to all my clients. It's a simple morning practice in which you do... well... nothing!

Mornings are precious — we are more likely to achieve "flow state" during this time — so it's best to capitalize on it when you can.

Wikipedia describes flow state as: "the mental state in which a person performing an activity is fully immersed in a feeling of *energized focus*, full involvement, and enjoyment in the process of the activity."

When we are in a flow state we are powerfully connected to our subconscious and are able to create transformation deep within our minds; time and space become irrelevant because we are so tuned in.

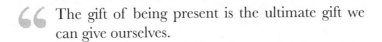 The gift of being present is the ultimate gift we can give ourselves.

The practice is simple and I've already introduced you to some of these questions in the last "reflection to action" challenge. For the first couple minutes of your day, just be. Sit in your energy and contemplate the following three questions:

1. How am I feeling today?

2. How do I want to show up for myself and others?

3. What can I do today that will make me feel more energized?

Really tune in with your body, your feelings, your needs, and your desires. Visualize as much as you can, breathe deeply and enjoy it. While it is a simple practice, it is truly powerful and building it will need discipline on your part.

Start with one or two minutes and eventually work up to spending fifteen (or even more) minutes on this exercise. Slow down as much as you can. Journal if you like, or simply visualize and say the answers out loud to yourself.

If you're serious about evolving, if you *truly* want to stop feeling like an overwhelmed dizzy mess, if you finally want to embrace your success and celebrate all that you are, if you want to show up energetically and powerfully in your life, *this* practice can get you started!

NINETEEN

On Health

"I promise you nothing is as chaotic as it seems. Nothing is worth diminishing your health. Nothing is worth poisoning yourself into stress, anxiety, and fear."

~ *Steve Maraboli*

You have to become obsessed with caring for yourself in order to generate the energy to show up fully and take responsibility for your life's direction. If you have productive energy you will have incredible clarity. If you manage your stress, you will be able to make decisions from a position of strength and positivity, not fear. Here are seven actionable steps to help get you on your journey:

Step # 1: Assess Your Stressors & Write Down How They Show Up In Your Life

Where does your stress come from? Take a few minutes and look at the areas of your life and the potential stressors they hold. Write down what happens when you are stressed. Do you have difficulty sleeping or staying asleep? Maybe you feel the need to drink wine to calm your nerves or you crave sugar and caffeine to get you going. Perhaps you have muscle aches and pains, especially in your neck, shoulders and back? This step is about creating *awareness* around where your stressors are coming from and how this shows up in your life.

Step # 2: Create A Vision For What Balance In Your Life Will Look Like

Once we take a step back and assess where our stress actually comes from, it's time to ask ourselves what we would like to experience instead. We spoke a lot about balance in this book. Go ahead and write down exactly *what* having balance looks like for you.

Step # 3 Let The Food Be Thy Medicine And Medicine Be Thy Food

Food is the most powerful medicine we have. But it can also cause *more* stress and take away *more* energy if we're consuming, quite frankly, crap. Eating the right food will help support your adrenal function which helps you feel more energized. Through my own journey I landed on the following:

• No single diet is right for everyone. What's healthy for one person may not be healthy for another.

• The body has an innate wisdom — listen to it.

• Diets are not useful as dogma, but they are useful as a reference.

A couple more quick tips on how to eat for energy...

1. Increase healthy fats: healthy fats from wild caught cold water fish, avocados, nuts and seeds or coconut oil have an incredibly positive effect on the body. They help you absorb vitamins, regulate hormones, and stabilize your metabolism.

2. Reduce and remove offenders: these are the foods that commonly cause digestive upset and stress out the adrenal glands (so they can take away energy). Remove refined sugar, focus on eating low-glycemic foods, reduce (or at least temporarily remove gluten) and any other foods that cause inflammation.

3. Eat the rainbow: there are important vitamins and minerals in all vegetables. Adding color to your plate will also lift you spirit.

Step # 4 Get Your Snooze

Sleep is a super powerful rebalancing agent! So, it's time to get serious and make sleep a priority. Low energy levels and poor adrenal function are often related to a lack of rest and sleep. A few tips for a great night sleep are:

• Introduce a *power down hour* before bed. No tech, just some tea, a hot bath and some essential oils.

• Use black-out curtains.

• Go to bed before 10:00 pm and get your 8 hours.

• Breathe deeply for at least 2 minutes before bed. You can try the "5-5-7" breath. Inhale for a count of five, hold for five, and exhale for seven.

Step # 5 Practice Mindfulness & Be Present

"We are living in a world of tomorrows."

~ Dr. Marcella Pick

When was the last time you paid attention to the smallest most habitual movement, like getting up from a chair? Starting to take note of the tiniest movements or behaviors can be a powerful tool in becoming more present and mindful. The key to this step is to retrain our brain to bring awareness back to what we do and what we accomplish each day. Being mindful and present will allow us to reduce stress and become more present *in the now* rather than racing to the next thing!

Tools For Mindfulness

• Meditate once a day. You can do this on your own or use an app like Calm or Headspace.

• Introduce silent minutes or journaling into your morning.

• Focus on the positive. Ask yourself: what's going well?

Step # 6 Adapt Your Movement

Not all movement is equal. If you feel drained after a heavy or intense workout it may be time for you to swap it for some calmer, slow moving options.

A simple walk or some yoga can be a great way to add movement without maxing out your body, and low intensity workouts in between your high impact sessions are proven to help you increase your endurance!

Extra tip: Go outside! Movement in nature will boost your mood *and* energy.

Step # 7 Perfect Just The Way You Are

The desire for perfection can take a heavy toll on our wellbeing! Perfectionism can completely zap our energy as we strive to hold ourselves to the high and often unrealistic expectations we set. It's time to let it go.

Making mistakes is the most human thing there is, so let's take a step back, cut ourselves some slack and become *perfectly imperfect.*

Perhaps next time you get dressed, put two different colored socks on. Just try it! Trust me, these small steps can help you break free from your perfectionism prison and access an abundance of energy!

Reflection to Action Challenge Part III

Let's finish your journey to achieving with grace strong! The third step in the SIE Coaching Model is "ENERGY".

This is the step that weaves it all together. *You* are your number one asset, if you take care of yourself, you can take care of others, your business, and be the brilliant leader you were destined to be.

I will end with a friendly reminder that you have to become obsessed with caring for yourself in order to generate the energy to show up fully and take responsibility for your life's direction. If you have productive energy you will have incredible clarity. If you manage your stress, you will be able to make decisions from a position of strength and positivity — not fear.

When we focus on doing things that energize us and let go of the stuff that doesn't, it's the most incredible needle mover you will ever experience.

The Energy Wheel

The Energy Wheel is a simple, yet powerful self assessment tool to visualize key areas of your life and will highlight where you most need improvement. It originates from what is called a "Wheel of Life" assessment that rates satisfaction of life in general. I use this frequently with my coaching clients. It only takes a few minutes to complete and it is an incredible self-reflection tool.

This visual representation of how energized you feel in each area will make it simple to gain the clarity around which area to focus on first.

Step 1: Draw a circle on a blank piece of paper. Then divide it into six areas:

• Career

• Finances/Money

• Relationships

• Spirituality

• Health

• Add anything you like, anything that feels important.

Step 2: Rate yourself on a scale from 1-10 in terms of how energized you feel by each of these areas right now (one being low energy and ten being fully energized).

Career 1-2-3-4-5-6-7-8-9-10

Money 1-2-3-4-5-6-7-8-9-10

Relationships 1-2-3-4-5-6-7-8-9-10

Spirituality 1-2-3-4-5-6-7-8-9-10

Health 1-2-3-4-5-6-7-8-9-10

Step 3: Put a dot on the circle for each corresponding area. The closer to the centre, the less energized you feel in this area.

Step 4: Connect the dots

Step 5: Look at your Energy Wheel now that you have connected the dots with lines. What do you notice? Which areas are currently energizing you and which seem to drain your energy?

Repeat the next 3 steps for each area that shows low scores (6 or less).

Step 6: Go back to the first step of the SIE Model - "What's the story you are telling yourself?"

Step 7: Now let's weave in step two of the SIE model - "How could you bring more Intention to this area?"

Step 8: Let's bring back the energy with step three of the SIE model: "What could you do to help you feel more energized in this area?"

What's a golden nugget you are taking away from Part III?

On Your Next Steps

"You only live once, but if you do it right, once is enough."

~ *Mae West*

We only have one life and it is up to us to make the most of it. As Graceful High Achievers, we have the ability to create powerful shifts and live a life that will far surpass us.

When we learn to manage our achiever self in a way that allows us to go after our biggest goals — but in a way that lifts us and others up — we become *unstoppable*.

It's up to us. We have a choice to make about how we want to spend this one life we have been given. Do we want to chase perfection and external validation — or do we want to start to lead from a place of strength, owning who we are and creating positive change? I believe that the world needs us now more than ever.

And the best part of it all — and something that I want you to remember — you do not need to lose a part of you to create the change you wish to see.

You can achieve amazing things with grace and ease. You *can* have it all, just not all at once.

When we learn to understand ourselves better than we ever have, we can lean into our strengths instead of focusing on our weaknesses. We can choose to bring energy to our days.

Growing up with a single mother taught me that to succeed in life I would have to work incredibly hard. I set out on a journey that yielded a lot of results, but I did it at the expense of my health, sanity, and happiness. While I still believe that it takes great effort to reach the next level of success, I learned that there is a *graceful* way to do it.

Life has changed substantially for me in the past few years but even more so in the past six months. I feel balanced, elegant, clear headed and strong. I am moving closer to my dreams each and every day. I'm crushing my goals, but I no longer feel I'm overly busy. I have more energy and more time than ever before while accomplishing everything I want.

And that my friend, has become my mission. I have a dream that every woman and girl out there will be able to achieve more with grace and ease. I believe that we can transform the world and create true balance. I believe that together we can inspire future generations to stop chasing external validation and start embracing and celebrating ourselves for who are are. The only question is, are you with me?

Hire Theresa

"You have to become obsessed with caring for yourself in order to generate the energy to show up fully and take responsibility for your life's direction; this starts by investing in your growth both personally and professionally. If you have productive energy you will have incredible clarity. If you manage your stress, you will be able to make decisions from a position of strength and positivity not fear."

~ Theresa Lambert

∾

Theresa is Certified Transformational Coach, Leadership & Mindset Strategist and Motivational Speaker. If you are ready to accelerate growth both personally and professionally for yourself, your team or organization, look no further. Theresa is the ideal person to deliver a keynote at your next event to inspire positive change.

To book Theresa to speak as a Coach or Consultant, contact:

Theresa Lambert
Theresa Lambert Coaching & Consulting Inc. Whistler, BC
604-906-1932
theresa@theresalambertcoaching.com
www.theresalambertcoaching.com

Acknowledgments

To those who have stood beside me, cheered me on, lifted me up, supported me, trusted me and extended a hand to help me get back up, Thank you! My journey to getting to know myself, expressing my crazy, owning my ability and achieving with grace would not have been possible without some incredible people that have been part of my journey. I am forever grateful to have such a loving and supportive group of people that surround me.

My wisdom and knowledge came over time, by embracing change and opening myself up to new perspectives, it came from taking risks, falling down and getting back up. There are so many people over my lifetime who's friendship, mentorship, love, energy, influence and guidance have had a significant impact on me and my growth. Even if you are not mentioned personally in this book, please know that if you've been a part of my journey over the past 35 years, I deeply appreciate you and will be forever grateful for your support. I share my deepest and most sincere thanks with my family & friends.

My husband Mike who always encourages me to keep going, loves me for who I am and to find a way to share his wisdom just at the right moment. Thank you to my Mom Sabine, who raised me to be a strong, independent and resilient woman and teach me that one of the most important things in life is to get back up and keep going.

To my bestie Paige Green who's always here for me and my sister Vera, my niece Elinor, step-dad Juergen and step brothers Niklas and Jannes and my extended family in England John, Peter and Joan and Australia Jan, Jen, Richard, Hannah and Mason and the rest of the crew - thank you for your support, love and guidance. You all have been an integral part of my Journey and a reason I was able to realize this long life dream to write a book.

A special thank you to my Business Coach Mike Skrypnek who helped me get this book written and published. To my awesome editor Genevieve Pardoe, who had patience with me and helped me tie all the ideas together and to Ruth Barrow for designing an amazing book cover.

Thank you to:

Carolyn Hill, Pamela Brian Bennett, Nancy Steward, Cathy Goddard, Blair Kaplan, Mike Skrypnek, Genevieve Pardoe, Yasmin Haufschild, Caroline Bagnall, Wendy Leggett, Donna Horn, Julie Pecarski, Joanna Jagger, Lindsey Turner, Tess Evans, Kenni R. King, Michelle Ratcliff, Melissa Pace, Joey Gibbons, Chalsi Goetz, Allison Castle, Megan Dell, Jennifer Campbell, Katherine Lazaruk, Dina Legland, Carly Scholz & Family, Robyn Ziebell, Susan Bain, Stacey Morgenstern, Carey Peters, Fiona Douglas-Crampton, Janice Hulse, Wayne Katz, Flora Ferraro, Rebecca Warren, Sendi Traviljani, Lisa Dalati, Brenda Holben, Ruth Barrow and Diane Hanna.

Words of Wisdom

"Beware of your thoughts for they become words, beware of
your words for they become actions, beware of your actions
for they become habits, beware of your habits for they
become character, beware of your character for it becomes
your destiny."

~ Diane Von Furstenberg,
The Woman I Wanted To Be

Resources To Dive Deeper

Get on the list

Add some mindfulness and mindset tips to your Inbox by signing up to my email at www.theresalambertcoaching.com

Going deeper

If you enjoyed this book and want more guidance on your path to forge ahead and achieve with grace, check-out my online courses and coaching at www.theresalambertcoaching.com

Connect

www.theresalambertcoaching.com

www.facebook.com/theresalambertcoaching

www.instagram/theresalambertcoaching

www.linkedin.com/in/theresa-lambert-855b6957

Books I recommend to help you on your journey...

Everything is Figureoutable, Marie Forleo

The Happiness Project, Gretchen Ruben

High-Performance Habits, Brendon Burchard

Think and Grow Rich, Napoleon Hill

Dare to Lead, Brené Brown

Light is the new Black, Rebecca Campbell

Atomic Habits, James Clear

You are a Badass, Jen Sincero

Miracle Mornings , Hal Elrod

The Energy of Money, Maria Nemeth

Copyright © 2020 Theresa Lambert

Achieve With Grace

All rights reserved.

Book Cover Design by Ruth Barrow - Whistler Creative

Editing + Formatting by Fallon Publishing, fallonpublishing.ca

Published by Theresa Lambert Coaching & Consulting Inc.

No part of this publication may be reproduced, stored in a retrieval system or transmitted in any form or by any means, electronic, mechanical, photocopying, recording or otherwise, without prior permission. For information about permissions or about discounts for bulk orders or to book an event with the author or his colleagues or any other matter, please write to theresa@theresalambertcoaching.com

Disclaimer: This book contains the opinions and ideas of the author and is offered for information purposes only.

The author and publisher specifically disclaim responsibility for any liability loss or risk personal or otherwise, which is incurred as a consequence, directly or indirectly, of the use and application of any of the contents of this book.

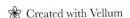 Created with Vellum

Made in the USA
Columbia, SC
03 August 2021

42740286R00095